LIKENESSES IN LINE

SCVLPTVRA IN ÆS.

Sculptor noua arte, bracteata in lamina   *Scalpit figuras, atque prælis imprimit.*

Ioan. Stradanus invent.

Phls Galle excud.

20.

Victoria and Albert Museum

LIKENESSES IN LINE

An Anthology of Tudor and Stuart Engraved Portraits

Harold Barkley
Department of Prints and Drawings

London: Her Majesty's Stationery Office

© Crown copyright 1982
First published 1982

ISBN 0 11 290352 5

Printed in England for
Her Majesty's Stationery Office
by Swindon Press, Swindon, Wilts.
Dd 696365 C60

Design by HMSO Graphic Design

Front cover
**Queen Elizabeth I
(1533-1603)**
Probably when aged about 62, *c* 1595.
Engraving by Crispin van de Passe I after a
drawing by Isaac Oliver.

Frontispiece
Engraving on copper. Plate 20 from the series
entitled *Nova Reperta*, published by Philippe
Galle, Antwerp [undated]. Engraved by Hans
Collaert (*c* 1530–1581) after Jan van der Straet
(Stradanus) (1523–1605).

E1247-1904

Contents

Introduction

This anthology of Tudor and early Stuart engraved portraits, with accompanying brief lives of the personages represented, is intended to provide characteristic examples of the engraved portraiture of the period and to enhance understanding of the history of Britain between 1550 and the death of James I in 1625. The majority of the prints included were produced in England, with the remainder coming from Antwerp and other cities in the Netherlands and from Germany. All are line-engravings, that is to say, each is printed from a copper-plate on which the lines constituting the portrait were incised by a tool called the graver. After completion of the engraving such copper-plates are inked and the required impressions are taken by passing each plate through a double-roller press, a process which has changed little from its earliest days.

The art of engraving was first developed in Italy, Germany and the Netherlands in the middle of the 15th century, but took another century to find its way into England. No work was produced here until the mid-16th century when the English did begin to practise engraving – at first only for portraiture and book-illustration – they learned their skills, not from the work of such outstanding earlier masters as Marcantonio Raimondi, Albrecht Dürer or Lukas van Leyden, but from minor engravers of Antwerp or Amsterdam often living as refugees in England because of their Protestant beliefs.

The history of the development of engraving in England is still only partially traced, despite the invaluable pioneering work of the late A M Hind. It is clear, however, that at first there were more foreigners than Englishmen engaged in the craft, the first English-born engraver being John Shute who died in London in 1563. He is not known to have engraved any portraits, but it is of interest to note that in the year of his death Queen Elizabeth saw fit to have a draft proclamation prepared directed against the production of unworthy portraits of herself. The portraits causing concern were clearly oil-paintings, but it was upon oil-paintings that most engravings were based. The draft voices the criticism that 'hitherto none hath sufficiently expressed the naturall representation of hir Majesties person, favor, or grace, but the most part have also erred therein'. It goes on to state that the queen will authorize 'some speciall person' to produce an approved image which may then be copied by others under licence and expresses a further intention 'to reform the errors already committed'. The Netherlandish engraving, possibly by Frans Huys, of the queen at the time of her accession (plate 3) is of a character which should have satisfied the queen's desire for a dignified presentation of her image, showing sufficient gravity, intimation of majesty and, on a personal level, a flattering emphasis on her elegant hands. The two later engravings of the queen by Crispin van de Passe I meet all the requirements of royal image-making, both being taken from approved portraits made by the celebrated limner Isaac Oliver. The one dated 1592 shows the queen half-length, seated, imperious and haughty, wearing the crown and bearing the orb and the sceptre (plate 4), while the memorial plate of 1603 (plate 5) shows her full-length, standing, a stiff, hieratic figure, again with crown, orb and sceptre and clothed in one of the elaborate, gorgeously embroidered and jewel-encrusted dresses which she favoured in her later years. In contrast, the portraits of Mary I and Philip II of Spain (plates 1 and 2) are straightforward renderings of formal, but non-state, portraits of the two monarchs. Elstrack's engraving of Mary, Queen of Scots (plate 6) is, like the portrait of Mary I, a later record made for historical purposes but in this case showing the sitter in majesty. An interesting variant in presentation may be found in the second portrait of Mary Stuart (plate 7) which is frankly a propaganda item, possibly by Hieronymus Wierix of Antwerp, issued to attract the attention of European Catholic sympathizers to Mary's pretended martyrdom. The portraits of James I and VI and of James with his queen (plates 9 and 10) were produced respectively in Augsburg and in Antwerp and represent foreign interest in the king before and after his accession to the English throne.

Two notable early engravers working in London were the brothers Franciscus and Remigius Hogenberg, born in Malines, who came to England about 1568 to join the book-production workshop established at Lambeth Palace by the learned Archbishop Matthew Parker. The type of work attributable to Remigius may be seen in the later portrait (dated 1582) of Sir Henry Brooke Cobham (plate 20). He also became an engraver of maps and was one of the half-dozen men – three foreigners and three Englishmen – employed on Christopher Saxton's great atlas of the English and Welsh counties engraved between 1574 and 1579 with the queen's approval and encouragement and published in the latter year. The publication was significant in that, prior to its appearance, the great majority of engravers working in England were foreigners but from then onwards the proportion of native-born engravers began to grow significantly.

It will be seen that two families constantly appear among the names of the engravers of the plates illustrated. These are the van de Passe family of Utrecht (headed by Crispin van de Passe I) and the Wierix family of Antwerp who represent respectively the Protestant and Catholic causes in terms of visual propaganda and who were instrumental in disseminating throughout Europe images of the heroes and heroines of their respective cults. Another notable name in England is that of Renold Elstrack, the principal executant of the fine series of 36 plates entitled *Baziliωlogia: A Booke of English Kings from the Conquest*, published in London by Compton Holland in 1618, from which the portraits of Mary I (plate 1) and Mary, Queen of Scots (plate 6) are drawn. Two years later, in 1620,

there was published jointly by the bookseller Jan Janson of Arnhem and the engraver Crispin van de Passe I of Utrecht the great series of 67 plates, commissioned by Henry Holland of London, entitled *Herωologia*. These plates, representing England's most famous and learned men, were engraved by two of Crispin's children, Willem and Magdalena. It seems likely that they were sent drawings on which to base their engravings, these possibly being supplied by their brother Simon who was the most accomplished of all the engravers at work in England during the reign of James I. Examples of plates from the *Herωologia* are the portraits of Sir Martin Frobisher (plate 32) and Thomas Sutton (plate 28). Portraits by Simon van de Passe are those of the Earl of Nottingham (plate 15), the Earl of Worcester (plate 16), William Butler (plate 26) and Sir Walter Ralegh (plate 34). There is also included a later re-engraving of Simon's solemn portrait from life of the Princess Pocahontas (plate 36). The elder Crispin van de Passe was the engraver of the 1592 portrait of Queen Elizabeth (plate 4), the portrait of Thomas Cavendish (plate 35) – taken from an engraving by Jodocus Hondius – and, possibly, the plate depicting the Gunpowder Plot Conspirators (plate 31). From this it will be obvious that there were still more foreign than native engravers at work for the English market in the early part of the 17th century.

Notable among English engravers around the turn of the century was William Rogers who was working during the last 14 years of Elizabeth's reign and of whom Hind remarks that he was 'the first Englishman to attain something more than a local repute in engraving'. His plates of Lord Burghley, the

Earl of Essex and John Gerard (plates 13, 18 and 25) demonstrate the growing proficiency of the English School, and as the new century progressed more English names began to appear on the scene, men such as John Payne, William Hole, William Marshall and Robert Vaughan. Their work lay principally in the production of small portraits, book-illustrations and title-pages. It seems probable that most engravers made their own drawings on which to base their engravings, taking the majority of their subjects from existing oil-paintings rather than from life.

The illustrations have been chosen to include, beside the sovereigns, princes, noblemen and statesmen, representatives of the Church, the law, literature, commerce and medicine as well as a group of naval commanders, navigators and explorers who so characterized Elizabeth's reign. Seven portraits of churchmen and theologians have been included to demonstrate the wide interest shown in the principal partisans in the acrid theological disputes of the age, the variety of deeply-felt religious belief, the consequent omnipresent character of the theological debate – with its strong political involvements – and the intense interest of the educated classes in its outcome. It must be remembered that throughout the 16th and 17th centuries political and religious controversies were indivisible, for with Spain, the Empire and France representing Catholic absolutism and the British Isles, the Netherlands and the North German states representing the Protestant mercantile opposition, faith and the national interest could not be safely distinguished by the individual citizen.

In addition to its religious and political ferments, the age was animated by intense intellectual, literary and commercial activity engendered by exciting opportunities for overseas exploration and development. It was a period of insatiable curiosity in all things spiritual and material, in the nature of God and His relationship to man, in the nature of the state and its government, in the discoveries of the explorers and their relevance to human needs and in the establishment of means towards the determination of scientific method. All around was stimulus, tension and excitement, and it is fair to say that virtually all the men and women represented in the illustrations contributed in some way towards the creation of the intellectual, moral and social climate of their times.

All but one plate of those used as illustrations are drawn from the superb collection of engraved portraits given by the late Edgar Seligman to the Department of Prints and Drawings in 1958.

It will speedily become apparent to the reader how indebted I was in preparing this book to the articles of many contributors to the *Dictionary of National Biography*, to the writings of the late A M Hind and the late Professor Sir John Neale and to those of the Director at the Victoria and Albert Museum, Dr Roy Strong.

List of works referred to in abbreviated form

O'D – O'Donoghue, F M: *British Museum. Catalogue of Engraved British Portraits*, 6 vols, London, 1908–25.

Hind: Part I – Hind, A M: *Engraving in England in the Sixteenth and Seventeenth Centuries, Part I, The Tudor Period*, Cambridge, 1952.

Hind: Part II – Hind, A M: *Engraving in England in the Sixteenth and Seventeenth Centuries, Part II, The Reign of James I*, Cambridge, 1955.

C and N – Corbett, M and Norton, M: *Engraving in England in the Sixteenth and Seventeenth Centuries, Part III, The Reign of Charles I*, Cambridge, 1964.

R S *Elizabeth* – Strong, Roy C: *Portraits of Queen Elizabeth*, Oxford, 1963.

R S – Strong, Roy C: *National Portrait Gallery. Tudor and Jacobean Portraits*, 2 vols, London, 1969.

List of engravers with biographical notes

Boëtius Adams Bolswert (*c* 1580–1633)
He and his brother Schelte (also an engraver) were the sons of Adam Uytema of the town of Bolsward in the Netherlandish province of Friesland. They assumed their working name from their place of birth. Boëtius worked first of all in Amsterdam, under the influence of Nicholas de Bruyn, but by 1612 he was in Haarlem and afterwards worked in Brussels. He was a member of the guild in Antwerp by 1620 and apparently continued to live in that city until his death in March 1633. He is best known for his engravings after Rubens and Abraham Bloemaert.

Dominicus Custos (post 1550–1612)
The son of the engraver and painter Pieter Baltens, he was born in Antwerp. He later assumed the name of Custos and moved to Augsburg in Germany where he was established by 1584. He worked in that city as both engraver and print-seller for the remainder of his career, although in 1607 he was in Prague, apparently in the service of the Emperor Rudolph II. He died in Augsburg in 1612.

Francis Delaram (worked *c* 1615–*c* 1624)
Probably of Netherlandish birth, it seems likely that he came to London a year or two before 1615, which is the earliest date to appear on his engravings. The date of his death is not known, but it appears that he was working as late as December 1624 when the betrothal took place of the Prince of Wales (later Charles I) to Henrietta Maria of France, an event recorded in one of Delaram's plates. He contributed four plates to Henry Holland's *Baziliωlogia* of 1618 and produced engraved title-pages and book-illustrations in addition to his 35 known portraits.

Martin Droeshout (1601–*c* 1652)
A member of a family from the South Netherlands settled in London. He was baptized at the Dutch Church in Austin Friars in 1601 and probably died about 1652. Besides his portraiture he produced engraved title-pages and book-illustrations.

Renold Elstrack (1570–post 1652)
Born in London, the son of a Netherlandish glazier, Elstrack's father is recorded as a member of the Dutch Church in Austin Friars in 1582–3. Elstrack was possibly a pupil of William Rogers and his earliest dated plate was published in 1598. He engraved the majority of the plates in Henry Holland's *Baziliωlogia* of 1618 and was altogether responsible for 65 portrait subjects and more than 40 engraved title-pages, book-illustrations and maps. He contributed two maps to Samuel Purchas' *Hakluytus Posthumus or Purchas his Pilgrimes*, published in London in 1625.

George Glover (worked *c* 1634–*c* 1652)
Glover's known engravings – more than 90 in number and including 42 portraits – extend over the period 1634 to 1652. Nothing is known of his life other than that which is implicit in his varied output.

Pieter van der Heyden (Petrus a Merica) (worked *c* 1551–*c* 1572)
Probably born in Antwerp. Working as an engraver for the famous Antwerp publisher Hieronymus Cock from 1551 to 1572 and first recorded as a member of the guild in 1557. He engraved mainly after Pieter Breughel, Hieronymus Bosch and other Netherlandish artists.

Remigius Hogenberg (*c* 1536–died *c* 1588)
Born in Malines (Mechlin) in Brabant, the son of a painter and engraver from Munich, he came to England with his brother Franciscus about the year 1568 at the invitation of Archbishop Matthew Parker to join the archbishop's team of artists and craftsmen established at Lambeth Palace. Besides a small group of portraits and book-illustrations Remigius is most notable for engraving nine of the maps which appear in Christopher Saxton's *Atlas* of England and Wales, published in 1579. His bird's-eye plan of Exeter is dated 1587.

William Hole (worked *c* 1607–died 1624)
Hole is known to have been working in London in 1607 as his engraved title-page to an

edition of the Genevan Bible was published in that year. He was appointed chief engraver to the Mint in 1618 and subsequently also became engraver of the king's seals. In a document of September 1624 relating to his office he is described as deceased. His varied output includes portrait engravings, title-pages, maps, engraved calligraphy and music. He appears to have had many friends among literary men and musicians. Stylistically his work is interesting in that it is related to French engraving rather than to the predominant Dutch and Flemish schools.

Jodocus **Hondius** (1563–1613)

Hondius (his vernacular name was Josse de Hondt) was born at Wacken near Thielt in West Flanders. He was educated in Ghent and as a young man was employed as an engraver by the Duke of Parma, Governor of the Spanish Netherlands. About 1583–4 he was obliged to flee to England on account of his Protestant beliefs and was employed in London as an engraver of maps and a maker of geographical globes and scientific instruments. His earliest dated English engravings are from 1589. He worked in England until about 1593 producing, besides his highly-important maps and globes, portraits of recent English monarchs. On his return to the Netherlands he settled at Amsterdam and involved himself with map-engraving and map-publishing. In his last years he was engaged on engraving the maps for John Speed's *Theatre of the Empire of Great Britain*, 1611–12. Hondius died at Amsterdam in February 1613.

Frans **Huys** (1522–1562)

Born in Antwerp, he was a member of the Guild of St Luke in that city in 1546. He worked largely as an engraver of paintings, particularly those of Frans Floris and Pieter Breughel, for the celebrated Antwerp publisher Hieronymus Cock. His work is sometimes confused with that of Franciscus Hogenberg.

Thomas de **Leu** (1560–1612)

Of Flemish or Northern French extraction (possibly from Beauvais) he was working in Paris from 1576 until his death, having begun his career in the workshop of Jean Rabel. He engraved many fine protraits, a great number being after portraits by his father-in-law Antoine Caron, and became the major French portrait engraver of his time.

William **Marshall** (worked *c* 1617–*c* 1650)

Nothing is known of Marshall's life. His first known engraving appeared in a book published in London in 1617. His work appears in publications supporting the loyalist cause issued between 1648 and 1650 and he subsequently disappears from the scene.

Crispin van de **Passe I** (1564–1637)

Head of the celebrated van de Passe family of engravers he was born in Arnemuiden, near Middelburg, on the island of Walcheren in Zeeland. He was living in Antwerp at the time of the capture of the city by Spanish forces in 1585 and later moved to Cologne where he lived until 1612. He then settled in Utrecht where he died in 1637. Although certain of his prints carry imprints for Paris, London and Frankfurt there is no record of him ever having visited London. Four of his children were well-known engravers. Of these Simon worked in England and it is

possible that his brother Willem also did so for a brief time.

Crispin van de **Passe II** (1593/4 or 1597/8–post 1670)

The eldest son of Crispin van de Passe I he was born in Cologne, the actual date of his birth being uncertain. Early in his career he was responsible for a celebrated book of flower engravings, entitled *Hortus Floridus*, which was published in 1614–15 at Utrecht and Arnhem, appearing subsequently in editions with Latin, Dutch, French and English text. He was later working in Paris on the plates for Antoine Pluvinel's important book on horsemanship, published in 1623 and entitled *Maneige Royal* or *Instruction du Roy à l'exercise de monter à cheval*. He continued to work for French publishers until at least 1628, apparently returning to Utrecht from time to time to assist his father. He settled in Amsterdam in 1643 and died there subsequent to 6th January 1670. He is not known to have visited England.

Magdalena van de **Passe** (*c* 1600–ante 1641)

Daughter of Crispin van de Passe I she was born in Cologne about 1600. She lived with her father in Utrecht from 1612 until her marriage. Her husband died in or before 1636 and she herself died before 1641. Her principal contribution to the history of engraving in England is her collaboration with her brother Willem on the 67 portraits engraved for Henry Holland's *Herœologia* published in London in 1620. It seems unlikely that she ever visited England.

Simon van de **Passe** (*c* 1595–*c* 1647)

Believed to be the second son of Crispin van

de Passe I born in Cologne about 1595. He appears to have been living and working in London from about 1612 to 1622-3, probably paying intermittent visits to his father in Utrecht during that period and to his brother Crispin in Paris about 1622 or 1623, when he engraved the author's portrait for Pluvinel's *Maneige Royal*. In 1631 he was appointed engraver to King Christian IV of Denmark and is believed to have been living in Denmark from December 1624. It is thought that he probably remained in that country until his death about 1647. He engraved nearly 60 English portraits, besides five title-pages and a map of New England, and he must be considered as the most important engraver working in England in the decade 1612-1622.

Willem van de **Passe** (*c* 1598-*c* 1637)

Third son of Crispin van de Passe I, born in Cologne about 1598 (or perhaps after 1600). If he was not resident in London it may be assumed that he visited the city from time to time from about 1620 onwards. His principal contribution may be found in his collaboration with his sister Magdalena in the production of the 67 engraved portraits for Henry Holland's *Herωologia* of 1620, towards which their brother Simon possibly contributed some of the original drawings from which the plates were engraved.

John **Payne** (*c* 1600-*c* 1640)

Born about 1600 he was associated in the early part of his career with both Simon and Willem van de Passe. His known output extends to about 50 engravings, often of considerable skill and reflecting his van de Passe connections. He enjoyed good professional standing in his lifetime and appears to have died about

1640, his last dated engraving being of 1639.

William **Rogers** (worked *c* 1589-*c* 1604)

His date of birth is unknown but he has the almost certain distinction of being the first English-born portrait engraver. His portrait of Queen Elizabeth as 'Eliza Triumphans' is signed and dated 1589 (the year following the defeat of the Spanish Armada). He is the outstanding English engraver of the Tudor period and worthy to be compared with the best of the foreign engravers working in England at that time. The rich ornament found in certain of his plates suggests that he was trained as a goldsmith as well as an engraver.

Robert **Vaughan** (*c* 1600-ante 1664)

As Vaughan's earliest known work is dated 1622 it is assumed that he was born about 1600, certainly of Welsh parentage. He is known to have lived and worked in London for many years, at a house in Fetter Lane, Holborn, and to have been devoted to the Royalist cause in the Civil War. Besides his many portraits (often used as book-illustrations) there are other plates in published works which indicate his antiquarian and alchemical interests. He was dead by 8 January 1664, the date on which his widow was granted permission to administer his estate.

Jean **Waldor I** (*c* 1580-*c* 1640)

Born in Liége about 1580. He worked at Nancy for the court of Lorraine, engraving religious subjects as well as portraits. He died about 1640 at the age of 60.

Wierix Brothers: Anton (*c* 1552-1624?); Hieronymus (1553?-1619) and Johan (*c* 1549-post 1615)

These three celebrated engravers were the sons of the Antwerp painter Antonie Wierix who was made master in the Antwerp guild in 1545 and who married in 1548. He lived and worked in Antwerp, as did his sons. Little is known of their lives despite the considerable position they held in the history of engraving in the Low Countries in the 16th century. Together they produced over 2000 plates and it is sometimes difficult to distinguish the work of each with certainty. All three studied the engraved work of Dürer and were considerably indebted to that master. Besides portraiture, the brothers tended to specialize in religious and allegorical subjects, secular subjects being uncommon in their output. They were devout Catholics and expressed the Catholic viewpoint in their work, just as that of the equally celebrated van de Passe family was devoted to the Protestant cause.

List of painters with biographical notes

Antoine **Caron** (*c* 1520–*c* 1600)
Born in Beauvais about 1520 he first worked in that city producing religious paintings and stained-glass designs. He was employed by Primaticcio between 1540 and 1550 to work on the decorations of the Palace of Fontainebleau and subsequently worked on designs for festivities on many royal occasions. He later became court painter to Queen Catherine de Médicis. In addition to his paintings and his designs for stained-glass he also produced designs for tapestries to be woven at the Gobelins factory and for book-illustrations. One of his daughters married the celebrated engraver Thomas de Leu. Caron died at Paris towards 1600.

John de **Critz** (ante 1552–1642)
Apparently born in Antwerp, probably the son of a Protestant goldsmith who was later obliged to flee from that city and who was established in London by 1552. In 1571 he is recorded as being apprenticed to Lucas de Heere, a Netherlandish painter then living in London. In 1582 he was in France in the service of Sir Francis Walsingham, buying pictures for his patron and visiting great country houses. He subsequently established himself as a portrait painter, employed by the court and the nobility, and secured the reversion to the office of Sergeant Painter to the king in 1603. He succeeded to the post in 1605. During his long career he worked on decorative schemes for many of the royal residences besides numerous projects relating to masques and theatrical entertainments. He died in London in 1642.

Hans **Eworth** (*c* 1520–post 1573)
Born in Antwerp he came to England about 1543. His early portraits are in the Antwerp Mannerist style but also show the influence of the School of Fontainebleau. He later showed indebtedness to the work of Anthonis Mor. Besides his portraiture he is known to have produced designs for pageants and masques and was the most significant artist painting in England in the mid-16th century. He is known to have been still working as late as 1573.

Marcus **Gheeraerts II** (1561–1635)
Son of the Flemish painter Marcus Gheeraerts I, who was working in England from 1568. He was born in Bruges, his father's native city, and came to England with his father, later becoming a pupil in London of the Netherlandish painter Lucas de Heere. He was later employed by his uncle John de Critz and afterwards established a considerable practice as a portrait painter to members of the court. He died in London in 1635.

Nicholas **Hilliard** (*c* 1547–1619)
He was born in Exeter about 1547, the eldest son of a goldsmith in that city. He was apprenticed to a jeweller and goldsmith but practised miniature painting from boyhood, being greatly influenced by the work of Holbein. He developed an extensive practice in London and was appointed limner and goldsmith to the queen about 1570, later making the second Great Seal of her reign. He must be regarded as the first great native-born artist after the Middle Ages but his successful career was clouded, nevertheless, in his later years by financial difficulties and a reduction in the volume of his practice; the latter probably caused by the success of certain of his pupils, notably Isaac Oliver. On the death of the queen, however, royal patronage was continued by James I. Hilliard wrote a treatise on the art of miniature painting which is of great interest for the light it throws on his working methods. He died in London in 1619.

Adrian **Key** (*c* 1544–1589)
Probably born in Antwerp about 1544, he was the nephew and pupil of Willem Key. By 1568 he was a master in the Antwerp guild and quickly established himself as a painter of portraits and religious subjects. He died in Antwerp in 1589.

William **Larkin** (worked *c* 1610–20)
Presumably of English birth, Larkin worked for distinguished clients during the second decade of the 17th century but very little is known about him. The Suffolk Collection at the Ranger's House, Blackheath, contains no

less than nine major portraits which may be attributed to his hand.

Michiel Janszoon van **Miereveld** (1567–1641)
Born in Delft in 1567, the son of a goldsmith. He was trained as a painter in Utrecht and Delft, establishing himself in a large practice. By 1625 he was a member of the Guild of St Luke in The Hague. He was portrait painter to the ruling house of Orange. Being a prolific worker he produced a multitude of portraits during the course of his long career. He died in Delft in 1641.

Isaac **Oliver** (ante 1568–1617)
Born in Rouen, the son of Pierre Ollivier, a Huguenot goldsmith or pewterer. He came to London with his parents about 1568 and studied miniature painting with Nicholas Hilliard. He travelled abroad, being in Venice in 1596, and became celebrated in England for the excellence of his miniatures and drawings. His clientele was distinguished, including Henry, Prince of Wales, the queen, Anne of Denmark, Sir Philip Sidney, the Earl of Dorset and other courtiers. He died in London in 1617.

Jean **Rabel** (c 1543–1603)
Born in Beauvais about 1543. From about 1575 he was established in Paris as a painter, engraver, writer and publisher. He was considered to be one of the best portraitists in France and was a court painter. He engraved religious subjects as well as portraits. He died in Paris in 1603.

Alonso **Sanchez Coello** (c 1531–1588)
Spanish painter of Portuguese parentage born near Valencia. By 1557 he was working for the Spanish court at Valladolid. He studied in Brussels and became acquainted with the celebrated Dutch master Anthonis Mor van Dashorst (called Antonio Moro) whom he succeeded as court painter to Philip II of Spain. He was a portrait painter of great distinction and was also responsible for part of the decorations of the Escorial. He died in Madrid in 1588.

Note: The museum registered number of the original engraving appears below each illustration.

1 Mary I
(1516–1558)

Engraving by Francis **Delaram** after a
painting of the School of Hans **Eworth**.
Plate to *Baziliωlogia, A Booke of Kings* . . . ,
published by Henry Holland, London,
1618.

(O'D 20; Hind: Part II, p.130, 22, 2nd state;
R S, p.213)

Mary, the third and only surviving child of
Henry VIII and his first wife Catherine of
Aragon, was born at Greenwich on 18
February 1516. She was brought up under
the care of the pious Countess of Salisbury
and was well educated in Latin, Greek, French,
Spanish, Italian, music and the mathematics
and science of the day. As part of her father's
foreign policy she was betrothed in 1518 to
the dauphin, son of François I, but political
circumstances changed and in 1522 she was
betrothed instead to her cousin, the young
Emperor Charles V, this engagement lasting
until 1525. In the same year she was made
Governor of Wales and became, in all but
title, Princess of Wales. In 1527 there was an
attempt to revive the earlier French engagement, this time to François I or to his second
son, the Duke of Orleans, but it came to
nothing.

As soon as the French ambassadors left
England, however, Henry embarked on his
scheme to divorce Mary's mother. It met with
considerable popular opposition, much of it
on Mary's account. She was recalled from
Wales and sent to live with her mother, her
court being broken up. The arrangement continued to the close of 1531 when mother and

daughter were separated as a matter of policy.
The divorce took place in 1532 and Mary
resolutely supported her mother, thus incur-
ring the displeasure of the king and the enmity
of his new consort, Anne Boleyn, especially
after the birth of the latter's daughter Elizabeth
(plates 3 to 5) in 1533. Mary was declared
illegitimate and deprived of her title of princess. She was removed to Hatfield to live
with her infant half-sister and was not
allowed to see her friends and supporters.
Her popularity in the country remained high,
so much so that the possibility of murder was
considered by her enemies.

In January 1536 Catherine of Aragon died,
Mary – to her great grief – being refused permission to visit her mother in her last illness.
With the execution of Anne Boleyn in May
1536 and Henry's subsequent marriage to Jane
Seymour the situation improved for Mary.
After great heart-searching she eventually sub-
mitted to her father, being reluctantly obliged
to acknowledge her bastardy and her father's
supremacy over the Church. After this her
circumstances eased and she travelled freely
from one palace to another. She showed herself to be warm-hearted and charitable and
was much grieved by the death of the amiable
Jane Seymour, a few days after the birth of
the future Edward VI in 1537. The rebellions
of 1538 once more put Mary in danger and,
over the next few years, she was to be sad-
dened by the execution of many of her old
friends and followers, including Lady Salisbury, her former governess.

The quest for a suitable husband was
renewed and among those considered were
the dauphin, the heir to the Portuguese throne,
the Duke of Cleves and Duke Philip of
Bavaria, the two last being Protestant candi-

dates. The collapse of her father's marriage to Anne of Cleves brought another change of policy and the abandonment of the schemes for Mary's marriage. In 1542, after the execution of Henry's fifth wife, Catherine Howard, the king made a final effort to marry Mary to the Duke of Orleans, but negotiations again failed. In 1543 her father married Catherine Parr, with whom Mary's relations were good. At this time war with France became inevitable and, to please the Emperor, Henry removed all Mary's remaining disabilities, her succession rights being restored by Parliament in 1544.

In January 1547, Henry died and Mary's young half-brother succeeded to the throne as Edward VI. Mary showed no envy and was affectionate towards both him and Princess Elizabeth. During her brother's reign she spent most of her time at one or other of the manors granted to her in her father's will. Marriage prospects were again under discussion in 1549 when Mary fell seriously ill, this putting an end to all negotiations. From May 1549 the Mass was prohibited in England and Mary's second great ordeal began. She refused to acknowledge the ban and continued to have Mass celebrated in her houses. The Emperor, Charles V, again intervened on her behalf and eventually an uneasy compromise was reached. In March 1551 she boldly appeared before the council, declaring that she would not change her faith. The Imperial ambassador later told the council that if Mary were further molested he would leave the country and war would be declared. Annoyances continued and the Emperor took steps to remove Mary from England to Antwerp. She was, however, well watched by troops and unable to leave her house.

On 6 July 1553 Edward VI died and the greatest crisis in Mary's life began. She was not immediately informed of her brother's death, the Protector Northumberland having forced the dying king to disinherit both Mary and Elizabeth in favour of his own daughter-in-law, Lady Jane Grey. He intended to arrest Mary, but she was warned and fled from Hunsdon in Hertfordshire to her house at Kenninghall in Norfolk. Lady Jane Grey was proclaimed queen on 10 July and Mary took refuge in Framlingham Castle, supported by the gentry of Suffolk and their tenantry. She soon had the support of 13,000 men and was proclaimed queen in Norwich on 13 July. More and more areas declared for her and the earls of Sussex and Bath, both members of the council, joined her at Framlingham on 16 July with an armed force. On 18 July rewards were offered for the arrest of Northumberland and on the following day the queen was proclaimed in London. Northumberland was seized at Cambridge and on 31 July Mary set out from Framlingham on a peaceful progress to London. On 3 August she was met by Princess Elizabeth and entered London in triumph.

She immediately restored Bishops Gardiner and Bonner to their sees of Winchester and London, making the former her chancellor and effective prime minister. Having endured much for her faith she was determined to restore Catholicism in England, but she proceeded with caution, promising that matters of religion should be settled by Parliament. She told a messenger from the Pope that she wished to restore both the Catholic faith and the Papal supremacy in England and that she would welcome the appointment of her old friend Reginald Pole, son of Lady Salisbury, as Papal legate.

Northumberland and two other conspirators were executed. Others tried with them were allowed to live, for Mary was reluctant to agree to any executions and showed no vindictiveness against her enemies, even refusing to allow the execution of Lady Jane Grey. On 1 October she was crowned at Westminster by Bishop Gardiner. The council wished her to marry as soon as possible and she consulted her cousin, the Emperor, on the subject. He proposed his son Philip of Spain (plate 2) as a candidate and Mary unwisely accepted the suggestion with gladness. The proposed marriage was unpopular in the country and both Gardiner and Pole advised the queen to show caution about such a marriage with an unpopular foreign ruler. Parliament recommended that she should marry a member of the English nobility, but Mary had already made up her mind to marry Philip. Negotiations proceeded rapidly against a background of popular dislike and as soon as the marriage articles were published in January 1554 three rebellions occurred, one led by the Duke of Suffolk in support of his daughter Lady Jane Grey, a second led by Sir Peter Carew in Devonshire and, thirdly, and most dangerous of all, the revolt in Kent led by Sir Thomas Wyatt. The first two were easily suppressed, but Wyatt was able to raise 15,000 men to march on London. The queen behaved with great courage, riding to Guildhall to address the citizenry as Wyatt was approaching London. His forces were eventually defeated and he was taken prisoner. Sixty persons were subsequently hanged in London and Lady Jane Grey, her husband and Wyatt himself were executed. Princess Elizabeth was accused of complicity in Wyatt's rising and was sent to the Tower. The rising persuaded Mary to proceed more rigorously with the restoration of the old faith and, in spite of the opposition, she resolved to marry Philip as soon as possible.

Parliament considered and approved the marriage treaty in April 1554 and Philip landed at Southampton on 20 July. The marriage was celebrated in Winchester Cathedral on 25 July and from the outset Philip's unpopularity was evident. His conduct, however, was very discreet and he intervened on behalf of Princess Elizabeth and was at least partly responsible for Mary's full reconciliation with her sister in the autumn of 1554.

At the end of November it was announced that the queen was pregnant and early in 1555 Parliament passed legislation restoring Papal authority in England. Soon afterwards came severe penalties for heresy and on 4 February 1555 the first Protestant was burned at Smithfield. In April arrangements were made for the queen's confinement, but the hoped-for pregnancy proved to be false. Philip, realizing that there was no hope of securing his own succession to the English throne, resolved to leave the country. Despite Mary's sorrowful protests he parted from her on 29 August.

After his departure Mary sought solace in her work of restoring the Catholic Church, even attempting to restore some of the church lands seized by the crown, although in very great financial difficulties herself. She got her principal bill through Parliament, despite considerable opposition, by the beginning of December.

The lord chancellor, Gardiner, died in mid-November and Mary herself experienced ill-health, involving considerable pain, as well as great sadness at the absence of her husband.

Philip remained in close touch with English politics and attempted to persuade Mary to force her sister Elizabeth into a marriage with Philip of Savoy. Elizabeth refused the match, Mary refused to use pressure on her and a quarrel ensued between Mary and Philip. In March 1556 Cardinal Pole became Archbishop of Canterbury as well as Papal legate and Mary's principal adviser.

Mary spent most of 1556 quietly at Greenwich, but visited and was visited by Princess Elizabeth. In March 1557, to her great joy, Philip returned to England. It was, however, only politics that brought him, for he was by now King of Spain and ruler in the Netherlands and hoping to involve England in his current war against France. Despite her poverty Mary agreed to intervene and war was declared on 7 June. An English army of 8,000 men was sent to assist Philip's forces in the Netherlands and 4 July the king left to join them. Mary was never to see him again.

In the autumn of 1557 the Scots declared war in support of the French and by the winter a French army was threatening the English-held port of Calais. The town's surrender in January 1558 caused Mary great distress, but there was no money available to send adequate forces to attempt its recapture. In January 1558 a new Parliament met and voted essential taxes, but much opposition was voiced to Mary's policies at home and abroad. By the spring she was again afflicted by a false pregnancy. She continued unwell, suffering from intermittent fever and dropsy and was prompted to make her will. In September she was greatly distressed by the news of the death of Charles V. In October her illness, probably a malignant tumour, returned with new force and, recognizing her danger, she added a

codicil to her will. King Philip, informed of his wife's ill-health, pressed for the recognition of Elizabeth as her successor in order to keep Mary of Scotland – now wife to the dauphin – off the throne of England. Mary spent her last days in ensuring recognition for her sister. She died at St James' Palace on 17 November and by noon of that day Elizabeth had been proclaimed queen. On 14 December Mary was buried in Westminster Abbey with full Catholic rites.

A high-spirited, stern-willed woman, Mary was praised in her early years for her good looks and personal charm. A long history of adversity, persecution and, finally, illness served to sour her character in her later years, but her great loyalty to her mother and her faith never wavered. Despite her recourse to persecution of her religious opponents she was personally kind and gentle towards children and her servants and charitable to the poor. She was always upright and honourable in her dealings and sought parliamentary approval for all her religious measures. However, she made her greatest mistake in marrying Philip of Spain, an act which alienated public opinion more than anything else she did in her reign.

The original painting by Hans Eworth from which this print ultimately derives was made in 1554 and this image, therefore, represents the queen about the time of her marriage, when aged 38. The actual painting from which it is taken is a version – not by Eworth himself – at Drayton House, Northamptonshire. The paper held by the queen is a petition by a certain Thomas Hungate.

D. PHILIPPVS II. CATHOLICVS, D.G. HIS-
PANIARVM, INDIARVM, ETC. REX, DVX
BRABANT. COMES FLANDRIÆ, ETC.

Anton Wierx fecit et excud.

2   E.3833–1960

2   Philip II
(1527–1598)

King of Spain; consort of Mary I of England

Engraving by Anton **Wierix** after a painting by Alonso **Sanchez Coello**.

Philip, the son of the Emperor Charles V and Isabella of Portugal, was born at Valladolid on 21 May 1527 and spent his childhood and youth in Spain while his father travelled throughout his widespread territories, incessantly dealing with matters of state and the direction of his armies. Philip was carefully educated and in constant receipt of advice from his father who impressed on him a realization of the high destiny to which he would succeed, imbuing him with a cold reserve and caution towards his advisers and councillors and a deep distrust of the nobility. He grew up proud, pious, self-opinionated and distrustful, essentially a solitary and lonely figure.

In 1543 he was married to his cousin, Mary of Portugal, who died in 1545. In 1554 his father decided that he should marry Mary of England (plate 1) in order to construct an alliance of Spain and the Netherlands with England in opposition to the territorial ambitions of France in the Low Countries. Through the abdication of his father in January 1556 Philip became King of Spain and possessed of all his father's territories in Europe and America.

His marriage to Mary proved childless and as Philip was intensely unpopular in England there was no chance of his exercising any claim to or influence on the throne of England at Mary's death in 1558. It suited him at that time to see Elizabeth (plates 3 to 5) as queen rather than Mary of Scotland, who was fully committed to the French interest. However, his victory over the French at St Quentin on 10 August 1557 and his subsequent marriage to the French princess, Elizabeth of Valois, in June 1559 reduced the threat from France while leaving him with the problem of a hostile England governed by a very able queen.

In 1561 Philip began his persecution of the Protestants in the Netherlands which so strongly influenced English opinion in further opposition to the power of Spain. In 1563 he began the construction of his lasting monument, the Escorial, an immense palace and monastery, which he built to fulfil a vow made after the victory of St Quentin. In 1571 his navy obtained a great victory over the Turks at Lepanto and in 1580 Spain's menace was further increased by the conquest of Portugal.

Philip's attitude towards Elizabeth developed from an early personal liking and admiration for his sister-in-law to a fierce enmity towards her as a heretic (she had been excommunicated in 1570), a friend of his insurgent peoples in the Netherlands and an instigator of piracy against Spanish shipping. In 1572 the Massacre of St Bartholomew in France served to confirm English opinion that the ultimate struggle must be between the Protestant states and their Catholic enemies and in the same year Drake led a marauding expedition against the Spanish Main. Circumstances led to a peace treaty and a renewal of trade between England and Spain in 1573, but Elizabeth continued to provide assistance to the Netherlandish Protestants, her principal aim being to ensure that neither France nor Spain could make strategic use of the Netherlands against England. In 1579 and 1580 the Papacy organized landings in Ireland (with some support from Spain) and in July 1580 Drake returned home from his voyage round the world with a vast Spanish booty. Elizabeth defied Philip's anger at this piracy and relations between the two countries continued to deteriorate. Without any formal declaration of war an English expeditionary force was sent to the Netherlands in 1585 to assist the Protestant rebels and in the spring of 1587 Drake attacked the Spanish fleet in port. Philip was so outraged that he determined to send his long-planned Armada against England at the earliest opportunity. His great fleet was shattered in July 1588, a disaster which effectively marked the end of Spain's real threat to England.

Philip died at the Escorial on 13 September 1598. His life had been one of great industry and single-minded application untouched by imagination or flexibility of policy. He constructed an unwieldy and slow bureaucracy, with himself sitting in total control at the centre of the spider's web, which soon ceased to be an effective instrument of government and proved in succeeding reigns to be a clog on all advance.

3 Queen Elizabeth I (1533–1603)

Birth to accession

Engraving of 1559, possibly by Frans **Huys** or Peter van der **Heyden** (Petrus a Merica).

(O'D 76 (Anon); Hind: Part I, pp.67, 68 (Huys); R S *Elizabeth*, Eng.1)

The future queen was born on 7 September 1533 at the Palace of Greenwich to Anne Boleyn, the second wife of Henry VIII. She was established at Hatfield in a separate household where she remained after her mother's execution in May 1536. Her parent's marriage was nullified, thus reducing her status to that of a royal bastard.

Much of Elizabeth's childhood was spent in the company of her elder half-sister Mary, the daughter of Catherine of Aragon, and her

3 E.2584–1960

half-brother Edward, son of Jane Seymour, the king's affection being bestowed on all three. In 1544 her position became more secure when she and her sister were re-established in the succession to the throne by Act of Parliament. She was very carefully educated by leading scholars of the day and became associated with the Cambridge humanists. Grindal and Ascham directed her studies in Latin and Greek and she also learned French, Italian and, subsequently, Spanish.

On the death of her father in January 1547 Elizabeth joined the household of the kindly Queen Dowager, Catherine Parr. The latter re-married and on her death in 1548 her widower, Thomas Seymour, Lord Sudeley, sought to marry Elizabeth. For this ambitious scheme he was arrested and eventually executed in March 1549. Sudeley's brother, the Lord Protector Somerset, himself fell from power, the new Protector being Northumberland. Throughout these perilous times Elizabeth remained unscathed, pursuing her course with customary discretion at either Hatfield or Ashridge.

Edward VI died on 6 July 1553 and Northumberland then attempted to place his daughter-in-law, Lady Jane Grey, on the throne. The conspiracy failed in the face of Princess Mary's determination and 12 days after her brother's death she was proclaimed as Mary I (plate 1). As a pious Catholic Mary was determined to restore the Papal supremacy in England, and Elizabeth prudently chose to attempt to secure her position by outwardly conforming to the restored faith, but her attendance at Mass was occasional and perfunctory. Wyatt's rebellion of January 1554 which Mary overcame with great courage, gravely affected Elizabeth's position, and on suspicion of complicity she was confined to the Tower from March to May 1554. She was then removed to Woodstock from where she maintained a running battle of wits with her sister and the Council.

After Mary's marriage to Philip in July 1554 there came a speedy reconciliation with the Papacy and with her sister. In April 1555 Elizabeth was brought to court at Hampton and after Philip's return to Spain in August she was permitted to remain with the queen at Greenwich. Her position became more secure as Imperial and Spanish policy favoured her succession, should Mary prove childless, rather than Mary of Scotland. However, in 1556 a Protestant plot came to light, intended to place Elizabeth on the throne in place of Mary, and members of her household at Hatfield were found to be implicated. At Philip's suggestion she was pressed to marry the Duke of Savoy but refused to consider the idea. In 1558 Mary was seriously ill and on 6 November was obliged by the Council to recognize Elizabeth as her successor. She died at St James' Palace on 17 November and Elizabeth, then at Hatfield, embarked on her long and glorious reign.

She was aged 25 and chose as her principal secretary Sir William Cecil (later Lord Burghley) (plate 13) who had held office under both Somerset and Northumberland in Edward VI's reign. She proceeded with great caution in matters relating to the Council and the Church, wishing to avoid alienating both Pope Paul IV and Philip of Spain and thus securing allies for Mary of Scotland who, as the strictly legitimate heir to the English throne, posed a constant threat to Elizabeth's security. Immediately after her succession she showed herself to the enthusiastic citizens of

London on processions through the city. Her coronation took place at Westminster on 15 January 1559 amid general rejoicing.

The engraving, of uncertain authorship, but clearly related to other known drawings and paintings, shows the queen as she was at the time of her accession, laying particular emphasis on her beautiful hands of which she was very proud.

4 Queen Elizabeth I (1533–1603)

Accession to armada

When aged about 58, c 1590
Engraving of 1592 by Crispin van de **Passe I** related to a drawing or miniature by Isaac **Oliver.**

(O'D 79; Hind: Part I, p.283, 2; R S *Elizabeth*, Eng.21)

Almost immediately after the queen's accession the question of her marriage arose. Various foreign princes and members of the English nobility were considered and rejected, for both a foreign match between equals and an English match with an inferior were likely to cause political difficulties. She was attracted to Lord Robert Dudley (plate 14), then the husband of Amy Robsart, but remained as always cautious, her discretion eventually proving master of her emotions.

Mary Stuart, Queen of Scots (plate 6) and Queen of France, by reason of her marriage to François II, constituted a major personal and Catholic threat and Elizabeth took

4   E.3000–1960

steps to support the Protestant opposition to Mary in Scotland. By the Treaty of Edinburgh of 1560 Elizabeth was recognized as the legitimate sovereign of England. However, on the death of François II in December 1560, Mary returned to Scotland and immediately became a direct threat to Elizabeth by refusing to ratify the Treaty of Edinburgh. Although Elizabeth was personally well disposed to Mary the danger she presented made it essential that Elizabeth should identify herself with the Protestant cause in France as well as in Scotland. In October 1562 Elizabeth became dangerously ill with smallpox and the question of Mary's claim to the succession became acute, for her Catholicism and lack of concern for English interests aroused great apprehension. Fortunately the queen recovered and then contemplated reducing the threat by arranging a marriage between Mary and her own favourite Dudley, now created Earl of Leicester. Mary, however, cherished the much more ambitious project of marriage to the son of Philip II of Spain. The queen attempted to meet Mary in 1564 to discuss their problems but again, as on two previous occasions, Mary declined and lost the possibility of a personal understanding between herself and Elizabeth.

On the failure of the proposed Spanish marriage Mary married her cousin, Lord Darnley (plate 8), in July 1565, giving birth to her son, the future King James VI and I (plates 9 and 10), in March 1566. The birth caused Elizabeth to consider again her possible marriage to the Archduke Charles of Austria, but prudence once more forbade a foreign and Catholic marriage.

The murder of Darnley in February 1567, Mary's subsequent marriage to Bothwell (followed by the latter's flight) and Mary's enforced renunciation of the throne of Scotland changed the situation yet again. Elizabeth as a sovereign was outraged by the deposition. She would have wished to see Mary still on the throne, safely under the tutelage of her Protestant lords and free from French influence. When Mary fled to England in May 1568 the queen kept her away from court and under close supervision. She also attempted to adjudicate charges brought against Mary of complicity in Darnley's murder but her commissioners failed to reach any conclusion. Elizabeth kept Mary in England but moved her from the dangerously Catholic and potentially rebellious North. Relations with Spain and France were extremely bad and war was feared, although Elizabeth and Cecil knew that neither country could risk such an involvement at that time. The northern Catholic lords were dismayed by the policies of Cecil and the queen and hoped for a marriage between Mary and the Catholic Duke of Norfolk. In 1569 the Earls of Northumberland and Westmorland rose in a vain and easily defeated rebellion, but the occasion provided Pope Pius V with an opportunity to excommunicate the queen in February 1570, thus releasing her Catholic subjects from their allegiance.

In Scotland the regent was murdered and matters came to a head between the supporters of Mary and those of her infant son. Elizabeth still wished to secure Mary's restoration, if at all possible, but her attitude changed radically with the discovery in 1572 of the Ridolfi Plot to secure by rebellion the marriage of Mary and the Duke of Norfolk. The queen reluctantly agreed to the execution of Norfolk but spared Mary, despite the great popular feeling which was shown against her. There was, however, now no possibility of Elizabeth taking any further action in support of Mary's cause.

The queen made a policy of keeping herself in the public eye and accessible to her subjects by means of annual progresses through different parts of the country and these journeys contributed enormously to her popularity. The continuing threat from the claims of Mary Stuart to the English throne caused Elizabeth to think again of marriage, this time to a French prince, but both the Duke of Anjou and the Duke of Alençon were eventually dismissed. The situation again changed with the Massacre of St Bartholomew, which profoundly shocked English Protestants and put back into power in France the relatives and friends of Mary Stuart. There was renewed pressure for Mary's death but Elizabeth instead sent a force into Scotland which captured Edinburgh Castle and effectively destroyed Mary's party. In March 1572 Burghley was made Lord Treasurer and Francis Walsingham, a deeply committed Protestant, became Secretary.

Trade was renewed between England and Spain in 1573, despite the marauding expedition of Drake (plate 33) in 1572. Although the queen sympathized with the Netherlandish Protestants then in revolt, she nevertheless wished to see Spanish rule maintained there, ideally through the native nobility, so that France was kept out of the Netherlands and Spain could not readily establish a base there for a major invasion of England. She was, however, quite prepared to see the revolt kept going with volunteer support from England.

Henri III (Elizabeth's former suitor Anjou) succeeded to the French throne in 1574 and Elizabeth, knowing him to be moderate, was able to intervene more effectively in the affairs of the Netherlands. The new governor of the Netherlands, Don John of Austria, wanted to secure peace, freedom to use his army against England and marriage to Mary of Scotland. Elizabeth thus had no option but to lend larger sums to the rebels.

After Don John's death in 1578 the queen again considered the possibility of marriage to Alençon, brother of the French king, who had previously been rejected as a suitor in 1570. Alençon saw such a marriage as a means of advancing his own ambitions in the Netherlands. Feeling in the country and the Council was, however, strongly against a Catholic marriage, especially in the face of renewed threats from the Papacy and Spain. In July 1580 Drake, having sailed round the world, returned home with great booty and the queen needed the support of France against an outraged Spain. She lent Alençon £30,000 for his Netherlands venture and in October 1581 he came to woo her personally. Popular opposition was too strong, however, and he was eventually bought off early in 1582 with a bribe of £10,000, returning to France where he died in 1584.

Mary Stuart meanwhile continued to give trouble with her constant intrigues to seize the throne of England and recover that of Scotland. Through her excellent intelligence service Elizabeth was kept informed of every new plot and the strictest vigilance was maintained. Mary continued to be treated leniently and, despite many grave anxieties, Elizabeth continued her vain attempts to reach an understanding and reconciliation. 1584 proved to be a year of alarms, with the expulsion of the Spanish ambassador after the revelation, through Francis Throckmorton, of Spain's

deep implication in the plotting against the queen and the murder in June of the Protestant champion, William of Orange. The powerful Protestant Association was formed in England to protect the succession against Catholic plotting; Mary quite failing to realize the extent of English hatred of her or to take warning from the belated discovery that her son James VI was unprepared to offer her any effective aid.

In January 1585 Mary was moved to Tutbury Castle in Staffordshire. In December 1585 a new Catholic contact was apprehended on landing in England and forced to become a double-agent. Mary was moved again to Chartley and, under the strict control of Walsingham, the head of the secret service, was allowed to receive and despatch messages from January 1586, via the French ambassador, all the correspondence being opened and read. In June Thomas Babington wrote to inform Mary of a plot to murder Elizabeth and on 17 July Mary wrote her fatal reply giving her warm approval to the plot. With this evidence Mary was arrested on 4 August. On 20-21 September Babington and 13 other conspirators were executed. Mary was taken to Fotheringay Castle in Northamptonshire where she was tried in mid-October. The evidence against her was damning but Elizabeth was only very reluctantly brought to agree to the inevitable verdict of 'Guilty'. In mid-November a deputation from Parliament asked for Mary's immediate execution and, after great heart-searching, Elizabeth published the sentence of death early in December, and on 1 February 1587 she reluctantly signed the death warrant. Burghley saw to its despatch before she could change her mind and on 8 February Mary was executed at

Fotheringay. There were great popular rejoicings in London but Elizabeth was filled with remorse, while the sovereigns of Europe were greatly shocked by the act. She blamed her secretary Davison for having acted too swiftly after her signature of the warrant and he, as scapegoat, spent 18 fairly comfortable months in the Tower in consequence. With the execution of Mary the Catholic threat to England was, inevitably, greatly reduced.

In the autumn of 1586 Elizabeth had sent an expeditionary force to the Netherlands under the command of Leicester and the war there became a constant drain on her limited resources. She did not wish to provoke Philip II too far but was, nevertheless, obliged to spend more money on building up her navy in case of eventual war with Spain. In the spring of 1587 Drake led his famous expedition against the Spanish naval ports inflicting great damage, and in the middle of May 1588 Philip finally despatched his long-planned Armada against England. Bad weather caused delay and gave the English good warning of the threat. Elizabeth, inspired by the challenge, threw aside all her customary prudence, visiting her army stationed at Tilbury and addressing them with such passionate intensity as to provoke instant devotion. In late July a great battle off Calais saw the defeat of the Spanish fleet and secured England's safety.

The engraving shows the queen as she was a year or two after the defeat of the Armada in the full height and glory of her reign.

POSVI DEVM ADIVTOREM MEVM

Miseren anno M I seri CorDIæ.

SEMPER EADEM

Nata Grenovici anno Christi MDXXXIII 6. 7d. Sept.

IVSTITIA

VERBVM DEI

ELISABET D.G. ANGLIAE, FRANCIAE, HIBERNIAE, ET VERGINIAE REGINA.
FIDEI CHRISTIANAE PROPVGNATRIX AÇERRIMA. NVNC IN DNO REQVIESCENS.

5   Queen Elizabeth I (1533–1603)

Armada to death

Probably when aged about 62, *c* 1595
Engraving by Crispin van de **Passe I** after
a drawing by Isaac **Oliver.**

(O'D 15; Hind: Part I, p.282, 1, 2nd state;
R S *Elizabeth*, Post.4)

The year 1589, following the triumphant victory over the Armada, was filled with sadness for the queen. Several of her old and trusted friends and servants died, including Walsingham and Christopher Hatton. She was also in severe financial straits because of the great costs involved in equipping the navy to face the Armada, paying her land army and continuing her support of Henri IV, now fighting to secure his succession in France against the forces of the Catholic League. Essex (plate 18) was appointed to the English command in France and his incompetence and irresponsibility combined with Henri's duplicity to cause enormous wastage of resources. The queen found herself obliged to sell crown lands and to allocate most of the proceeds accruing to the crown from privateering against the Spaniards to meet the vast expenditure incurred. Essex became the queen's principal favourite, after the disgrace of Ralegh in 1592 (plate 34). Elizabeth had no illusions about the rashness and ambition of her new favourite and saw to it that all real political decisions rested with herself and her trusted Cecil advisers.

By 1596, after the military success of the Cadiz expedition, Essex's reputation was at its highest and in 1597 the queen wished him to command a new expedition intended to destroy in its ports a new Armada which was then in preparation and to seize the Spanish treasure in the Azores. However, the so-called Islands Voyage failed completely in its main objectives and the queen was put to further annoyance by a bitter quarrel between Essex and Ralegh, who had served as a subordinate commander on the expedition.

In 1598 Henri IV made peace with Spain, an act which caused Elizabeth and her ministers to consider the possibility of a similar peace, despite Essex's fierce opposition, but in August the aged Burghley died and his death was soon followed by that of Philip II of Spain.

Sorely troubled by the rebellion in Ireland Elizabeth sought to appoint a new commander, hoping to avoid nominating Essex for the post. The latter's ambition was too great, however, and he demanded and eventually secured the post for himself, also extorting from the queen an army of 16,000 foot-soldiers and 1,300 cavalry. His boasting and insolent nagging of the queen made anything less than total success in the venture unthinkable. As things turned out his incompetence and disregard of orders caused total failure and in his desperation Essex committed the extreme folly of negotiating a truce with the rebel Earl of Tyrone. Elizabeth was, as usual, kept fully informed of events by her agents and when Essex, totally disregarding his explicit orders, returned to England to confront the queen she had him arrested. Robert Cecil and Francis Bacon (plate 30) were able to dissuade the queen in February 1600 from having Essex brought to trial. There was a spate of propaganda on behalf of the popular 'hero'

which further angered the queen and in order to vindicate herself before public opinion it was decided to bring Essex before a special commission of councillors and other leading figures. He threw himself on the queen's mercy but was nevertheless suspended from the exercise of his various high offices. In his continuing folly he indulged in treasonable attempts to involve James VI of Scotland and Lord Mountjoy, his successor in Ireland, in efforts to restore his former position. All this, of course, was well-known to the queen through her formidable intelligence service. Once more she followed her celebrated precept of *Video et taceo* (I see and keep silent), but at Michaelmas refused to renew Essex's valuable grant of the duties on sweet wines, allowing them to revert to the crown.

In February 1601 came Essex's ultimate madness when he attempted to persuade the citizenry of London to rise on his behalf. The queen, well aware of what was afoot, took steps to see that the attempt failed dismally. Essex was arrested again and speedily brought to trial, the queen being fully resolved on this occasion. He was executed in the Tower on 25 February, but only five others were executed as well, the queen allowing her customary horror of bloodshed to temper her justice and to cause her to show mercy to those who might reasonably have expected to die. Nevertheless, for some time after the execution Elizabeth and her councillors were obliged to practice a cautious vigilance until popular feeling was stabilized.

Money problems made it imperative that another Parliament should be summoned to provide funds for the continuing Irish campaign and to repulse a Spanish landing in Ireland made in September 1601. The new

Parliament, meeting in November, voted the necessary taxes but went on to attack the system of monopolies, so that the queen was obliged to promise some reform of the evils of the system. Meanwhile, in Ireland, Mountjoy was waging an effective campaign against the rebel Tyrone and the Spaniards, eventually defeating both at Kinsale on 24 December 1601.

By now the queen was very conscious of her age and while she had no doubts that James VI should succeed her on the throne of England she prudently avoided making any public declaration on the subject. Although generally her health was good she was given to melancholy at times. Christmas of 1602 was spent at Whitehall and late in January the court moved to Richmond. Throughout February the queen was out of sorts and further depressed by the death of her old friend Lady Nottingham. She fell ill, becoming feverish, unable to sleep and unwilling to eat. Her condition continued to deteriorate and she eventually died peacefully in the early morning of 24 March 1603, having previously performed her last royal duty by nominating James of Scotland as her successor.

This memorial engraving of the queen in majesty is based on the Isaac Oliver drawing at Windsor Castle, which seems in turn to derive from the state portraiture of the 1590s, such as the 'Ditchley' portrait of c1592 by Marcus Gheeraerts II and the later 'Procession' portrait at Sherborne Castle. It commemorates the queen in her favoured ceremonial costume of that decade, with wide farthingale, rich fabrics, many jewels, the orb and sceptre and the crown set on her great wig – the whole displaying an intentionally overwhelming magnificence.

6 E.758–1960

6 Mary, Queen of Scots (1542–1587)

Engraving by Renold **Elstrack**, probably based on a portrait derived from a miniature by Nicholas **Hilliard**. Plate to *Baziliωlogia, A Booke of Kings . . .* , published by Henry Holland, London, 1618.

(O'D 25; Hind: Part II, p.132, 24)

Mary, the daughter of James V of Scotland and his French wife Mary of Guise, was born on 7 or 8 December 1542 at Linlithgow Palace. Her father died only a few days after her birth and the infant queen and her mother moved to the security of Stirling Castle in July 1543. Mary was crowned at Stirling by Cardinal Beaton on 9 September 1543 and negotiations soon began for her betrothal to the Dauphin of France. When an agreement was finally reached she travelled to France in August 1548 and was brought up at the French court in strict accordance with her royal rank. She was married to the dauphin on 24 April 1558 and on the death of Mary I of England – ignoring the fact of Elizabeth's succession – she assumed the titles of Queen of England and Ireland in addition to her own. Her husband succeeded to the French throne as François II in July 1559 but his early death in December 1560 left Mary in a desperately weak position, with her influence in France gone and her prospects in Scotland poor. Her mother, the queen dowager, who had ruled as regent had died in June 1560 and Mary's kingdom appeared to be almost irrecoverable. Protestantism was triumphant, Catholicism forbidden and the crown of Scotland had already been offered to Elizabeth in exchange for her marriage to the Earl of Arran. Elizabeth refused this offer at about the time of François' death and the two events thus led to a revival of Scottish hopes centred on Mary.

After complex negotiations with her Scottish nobility and with Elizabeth, Mary left France for Scotland, landing at Leith on 19 August 1561. She was received with popular joy tempered by deep suspicion of her religious intentions. She declared herself ready to concede religious toleration, but her first concern was to secure from the Protestants toleration for her fellow-Catholics. However, her personal charm and geniality influenced opinion in her favour and her government was conducted by two trusted Protestants, Lord James Stuart (Mary's illegitimate half-brother, later Earl of Moray) and William Maitland. Opportunities to meet Queen Elizabeth were discussed but – in the light of later events – unfortunately proved abortive.

Mary was obliged to consider the question of re-marriage. Candidates such as King Eric IV of Sweden and the Earl of Arran were rejected, Mary finally deciding that Don Carlos, son of Philip II of Spain (plate 2), was her favoured choice largely because of the powerful influence to be obtained through an alliance with Spain. In March 1563 secret negotiations for such a marriage were begun but Catherine de Médicis' and Mary's Guise relations were bitterly opposed to such an alliance with Spain, dissuading the Pope and, ultimately, Philip II from approving the match. Mary was greatly disappointed at the outcome. She rejected the further suggested candidatures of the Archduke Charles of Austria and Robert Dudley, Earl of Leicester (plate 14), and resolved instead to marry her cousin Lord Darnley (plate 8), largely for considerations of political advantage based on his own strong claim on the succession to the English throne and his Catholic leanings. The proposed marriage caused great jealousy and dissension among the Scottish nobility, but Mary was determined and the marriage took place at Holyrood on 29 July 1565. Moray led a revolt against his half-sister the queen but was defeated by troops led personally by Mary and was obliged to escape to England.

Mary was now committed to restoring Catholicism in Scotland and to securing absolute power for herself. Her plans were ruined, however, by a quarrel with her husband over her refusal to bestow on him the crown matrimonial and over the favour which she showed towards her secretary Riccio. The murder of Riccio, the subsequent flight to Dunbar with Darnley and her heavy reliance on the aid of the Earl of Bothwell to effect her re-entry into Edinburgh put all her plans to ruin. She gave birth to her son James (plates 9 and 10) on 19 June 1566. Her discovery of Darnley's deep involvement in the murder of Riccio caused the marriage to disintegrate completely, leading to Mary's fatal liaison with Bothwell and the murder of Darnley on 10 February 1567. Public suspicion as to her involvement in the murder was general and little attempt was made to deny it. At a rigged trial Bothwell was formally acquitted of complicity and soon afterwards obtained a divorce from his wife. In mid-April Mary was abducted to Dunbar Castle, a stratagem agreed with Bothwell in advance both to protect her person and to provide some justification of implied pressure for the intended marriage. The ceremony took place – according to the Protestant rite – in Edin-burgh on 15 May. Bothwell's actions aroused the fear and jealousy of his fellow-nobles who attacked him at Borthwick Castle on 10 June, forcing him and the queen to flee to Dunbar. On 15 June the royal forces avoided battle at Carberry Hill and Bothwell fled abroad while the queen surrendered to her enemies. The nobles wished to secure the divorce of the queen from Bothwell, but she would not consent. She was imprisoned at Lochleven Castle and eventually agreed to abdicate in favour of her son, an act finally achieved on 24 July 1567, her half-brother Moray being named as Regent.

The queen escaped from Lochleven on 2 May 1568, but her supporters were defeated at Langside on 13 May and she finally crossed into England, landing at Workington, on 16 May. Mary immediately sought Elizabeth's protection, but the latter, while outraged at Mary's forced abdication, was cautious in her response, having Mary closely guarded although treated with all the respect due to her rank. Mary's request for an interview with Elizabeth was refused until the question of Mary's complicity or otherwise in the murder of Darnley had been resolved. English enquiries into the conduct of Mary and her accusers returned a non-committal answer but she, nevertheless, remained a captive.

Early in 1569 Mary was put in charge of the Earl of Shrewsbury at Tutbury Castle in Staffordshire. She was moved from there to Wingfield Manor but an attempted rescue caused her to be taken back to Tutbury. The English proposal that she should marry the Duke of Norfolk stimulated the revolt of the Catholic Earls of Northumberland and West-morland which resulted in the imprisonment of Norfolk and in Mary being placed in stricter confinement at Coventry. She was subsequently back at Tutbury and then at Chatsworth before being taken to Lord Shrewsbury's principal seat at Sheffield Castle in the autumn of 1570. There she remained, with only short breaks, for the next 14 years, until her gaoler was at last permitted to give up his charge.

The Regent Moray was assassinated in January 1570, this arousing fresh hopes of a Catholic revival in Scotland. The Norfolk marriage scheme was pursued, the position being clarified by the Papal dissolution of Mary's marriage to Bothwell, but the project was totally destroyed by the discovery in 1572 of the Ridolfi Plot to secure Mary's marriage to Norfolk through rebellion. Norfolk was executed and Mary became the object of even greater suspicion in Elizabeth's eyes. The English Parliament went so far as to recommend that Mary be executed but Elizabeth refused. After the Massacre of St Bartholomew in August 1572 English opinion against Mary hardened even further and she was strictly imprisoned until the capture of Edinburgh Castle in May 1573 ensured the virtual collapse of her cause. Conditions then became easier for her and, despite her detention, she was well treated on Elizabeth's orders and allowed adequate sums for her household expenses.

For the rest of her life Mary maintained a devious course of plotting and subterfuge. Ostensibly ingratiating towards Elizabeth and her ministers she was continually involved in negotiations with the Pope and Philip of Spain for the invasion of England and the capture of her son, to effect her liberation and the restoration of her throne. Elizabeth's highly efficient intelligence service kept her informed of developments in Mary's conspiratorial activities and early in 1585, after the alarms of the previous year, she was again subjected to more rigorous supervision at Tutbury Castle. In January 1586 she was removed to Chartley, also in Staffordshire, almost certainly to enable her to become more easily involved in the final conspiracy which led to her death. There, under the secret supervision of Walsingham, she was permitted to receive and despatch messages, via the French ambassador, all her supposedly secret correspondence being opened and read. In June Thomas Babington wrote to inform her of a plot to murder Elizabeth and on 17 July Mary wrote her fatal reply giving her warm approval to the plot. On 4 August Mary was arrested and her papers seized. Events then moved inexorably forward to her execution at Fotheringay six months later (plate 7).

This engraving, made for a publication issued 30 years after her death, appears to be based on the monument to the queen by Cornelius and William Cure which her son caused to be erected in Westminster Abbey between 1606 and 1612 over the spot to which her body was finally brought in October 1612.

7 Mary, Queen of Scots (1542–1587)

Trial and execution

Engraving possibly by Hieronymus **Wierix** after Thomas de **Leu** and Antoine **Caron**.

(Not in O'D)

7 E.4660–1960

At the time of her arrest on 4 August 1586 Mary was with a hunting party at Tixall Park and was detained there until all her papers at Chartley had been seized and searched. On 25 September, after the execution of Babington and his fellow-conspirators, she was taken to Fotheringay Castle in Northamptonshire where her trial on charges of conspiracy to procure the invasion of England and the death of the queen took place on 14–15 October. Mary defended herself with energy and skill, but the evidence against her was conclusive and although the 36 specially appointed commissioners had been forbidden by Elizabeth to proceed to judgment at Fotheringay they had, on their return to London, no alternative – even had they so desired – but to reach a speedy and unanimous verdict of 'Guilty' and to sentence Mary to death. On 12 November both Houses of Parliament petitioned the queen for the early execution of the sentence. Elizabeth hesitated, not wishing to incur personally the international odium of Mary's death. She clearly recognized the necessity but recoiled from the act and if any other adequate solution could have been found she would gladly have agreed to it. In fact the idea of assassination as an alternative to the scandal of the execution of an anointed monarch was discussed and abandoned. In the face of mounting pressure from Parliament, Burghley and the Council the queen gave way and on 2 December finally published the sentence on Mary, an announcement which caused great public rejoicing in London.

On 16 November Elizabeth had written to Mary, warning her of the sentence, Parliament's petition and the likelihood of early execution. Mary refused to change her response, denying the crimes with which she had been charged and refusing to make any submission or to ask for pardon. Facing her fate with great courage and resolution she was determined that the world should see her death as a royal martyrdom for the Catholic faith. Her son James VI interceded vigorously for her, as did the French ambassador, but without success. The internal situation in England was, in fact, so unsettled and excitable that Elizabeth could not afford to delay any longer and on 1 February she reluctantly signed the death-warrant. Burghley saw to it that the eagerly awaited document was immediately despatched to Fotheringay and on 7 February Mary was told that her execution had been fixed for the following morning. She remained perfectly calm at the news, spending most of the night in prayer.

At eight o'clock on the morning of 8 February she was brought to the hall of the castle, where the scaffold had been erected, and was prepared for execution. Her old gaoler, Lord Shrewsbury, was present as one of Queen Elizabeth's two commissioners. Mary wept at parting from her loyal servants but otherwise remained unmoved by the imminence of death and by the Protestant exhortations of the Dean of Peterborough. She went to her death calmly and with dignity and afterwards her body was embalmed and remained in state at Fotheringay until 1 August, when, by Elizabeth's command, she was accorded a royal burial in Peterborough Cathedral. After his accession to the English throne her son James had Fotheringay demolished and commissioned a splendid tomb in Westminster Abbey to which his mother's remains were removed in October 1612 to lie – with the irony of history – next to those of Elizabeth.

This memorial engraving, by a member of the Wierix family of engravers in Antwerp (a family devoted to the Catholic cause), was published at Antwerp soon after the execution. The image of the queen is copied in reverse from the well-known engraved portrait by Thomas de Leu, which was itself probably based upon a drawing by de Leu's father-in-law, Antoine Caron. The scene depicting the actual beheading of the queen formed the subject of a memorial painting known to have been commissioned by Elizabeth Curle, one of the two women in attendance on the queen at the end. She went into exile in Antwerp and it has been suggested that she may also be associated with this print, possibly being represented as the woman prominent in the foreground of the execution scene.

8 Henry Stuart, Earl of Ross, 1st Duke of Albany (1545–1567) (Popularly styled Lord Darnley)

Consort of Mary, Queen of Scots

Engraving by Renold **Elstrack**, apparently based on a lost painting.

(O'D 12; Hind: Part II, p.171, 13, 1st state; R S, p.61)

Henry Stuart, son and heir apparent of Matthew Stuart, 4th Earl of Lennox and his wife Lady Margaret Douglas (daughter of the 6th Earl of Angus by Princess Margaret Tudor, daughter of Henry VII of England), was born on 7 December 1545 at Temple Newsam,

near Leeds, Yorkshire, and was accorded the courtesy title of Lord Darnley by which he is best known to posterity. He was educated privately and was well trained in the manly arts, in which he became proficient.

In 1559 he was sent to France by his mother, soon after the marriage of the French king, François II, to Mary, Queen of Scots (plate 6), and he again visited France soon after the death of François in 1560. In the event of Elizabeth dying childless he had a claim to the throne of England through his grandmother and it is clear that his ambitious mother envisaged a possible union of the thrones of England and Scotland through the marriage of Mary to her son. The widowed Mary, however, was more interested in the possibility of a marriage with a Spanish prince. On the Spanish negotiations coming to nothing Mary returned to Scotland and Lady Lennox began the attempt to bring about a marriage between the queen and Darnley. In England Queen Elizabeth became suspicious of such intrigues and summoned Darnley and his mother to London in November 1561. They were placed in confinement for a while but towards the end of 1562 they were released and apparently received into the royal favour, Darnley frequently performing on the lute before the queen. In 1564 the Earl of Lennox, who had also been arrested, was released from the Tower and allowed to travel to Scotland in September of that year, although at this time Elizabeth was promoting the idea of a possible marriage between her favourite the Earl of Leicester (plate 14) and Queen Mary. Darnley was also permitted to leave London for Scotland in February 1565 when he immediately paid his respects to the queen at Wemyss Castle. She appeared to be struck by the appearance of the tall well-proportioned young man – despite his somewhat girlish face. Darnley appears to have felt little – if any – attraction to Mary. However, family ambitions prevailed and, despite apparent incompatibility of temperaments, negotiations for the match went ahead, Mary giving them her full support.

On 15 March 1565 Darnley was knighted and created Earl of Ross. On 22 July a Papal dispensation for the marriage arrived and on the same day Darnley was created Duke of Albany. The marriage took place at Edinburgh in the chapel of Holyrood House on 29 July, the bridegroom and his father both having ignored an urgent summons from Queen Elizabeth to return to England. Darnley's imprudent behaviour quickly made him unpopular. He chose disreputable companions, displayed great pride and did not attempt to hide his dislike of the powerful Earl of Moray, the queen's illegitimate half-brother and leader of the Protestant faction in Scotland. In every way he showed himself to be of low intellect, intemperate and reckless, so that Mary soon found him totally unsuitable as a consort, too untrustworthy to share confidences and incapable of assisting her in political decisions. She found it necessary to refuse to share the crown with him and turned more and more to her trusted Italian secretary David Riccio who had greatly assisted her in bringing about the unfortunate marriage. Her confidence in Riccio and her obvious lack of confidence in himself was deeply resented by her husband and there were many only too ready to encourage him in misconstruing the situation. A plot was hatched to assassinate the envied and hated Riccio, using the duped Albany as a figurehead in his role of betrayed husband.

He was also encouraged in his support for the plot by the promise of the conspirators – many of them being his relatives – to instal him as the head of the government.

Riccio was murdered on 9 March and Albany immediately gave the queen details of those concerned in it, without disclosing his own part in the plot, and assisted her to make her escape from Holyrood to Dunbar. He hoped by these means to recover favour with Mary in order to secure his rightful place as joint sovereign of Scotland. For a time their relationship became cordial but early in April the queen learned the truth of Albany's deep involvement in the murder plot. This effectively ended their marital relationship, despite an attempted reconciliation in June immediately prior to the birth of their son James, later to be James VI of Scotland and James I of Great Britain (plate 9). Albany found himself increasingly isolated, despised alike by the Catholic and the Protestant nobility, and in a mood of fierce resentment he began to contemplate leaving the kingdom. On 29 September he came to Holyrood to bid farewell to the queen. His father and the French ambassador succeeded in persuading him to postpone his departure and he paid another visit to his wife on 28 October while she was lying ill at Jedburgh. During that visit his arrogant behaviour to the assembled nobility sealed his fate. A conference of the nobles was held at Craigmillar Castle, near Edinburgh, where it was decided unanimously that Albany must be got rid of. He was at Stirling at the time of his son's baptism but did not attend the ceremony or any of the festivities. On learning that a pardon had been granted to the murderers of Riccio he made up his mind to quit the country as soon as possible and went to Glasgow with the intention of sailing from there. Before he could leave, however, he fell ill and the queen sent her own physician to attend him. When he was convalescent she came to visit him and induced him to return with her to Edinburgh.

In Edinburgh Albany was lodged in a somewhat isolated dwelling called Kirk o'Field. The house was blown up early in the morning of 10 February 1567 by a group of conspirators led by the queen's new lover James Hepburn, 4th Earl of Bothwell. The bodies of Albany and his servant were afterwards found in a garden some little distance from the explosion. They were apparently uninjured and it is assumed that they were strangled before the explosion by those who were responsible for it. On 14 February Albany was buried privately in the chapel of Holyrood House.

Although tall and physically attractive Albany had little else to recommend him, apart from his birth. His marriage to Mary was clearly dictated by supposed self-interest and family ambition, whilst on her side some degree of physical attraction merely served to strengthen her calculated decision to make the match for the sake of its apparently favourable implications for the increased stability of the throne and the aggrandisement of the dynasty.

The engraving, apparently based on a lost painting, shows Albany wearing the robes and chain of the French order of St Michel.

9 James I of England and VI of Scotland (1566–1625)

From his birth to his accession to the English throne

Engraving by Dominicus **Custos**. Plate to *Atrium Heroicum Caesarum*, Augsburg, 1600–02.

(O'D 2, 1st state)

James, the son of Mary, Queen of Scots (plate 6) and Henry Stuart, Lord Darnley, Duke of Albany (plate 8), was born in Edinburgh Castle on 19 June 1566 and succeeded to the throne of Scotland on 24 July 1567 on the forced abdication of his mother. He was crowned at Stirling on 29 July and placed in the care of the Earl and Countess of Mar with the Earl of Moray, his uncle, serving as Regent. He was carefully educated by a group of presbyterian ministers from whom he acquired considerable learning and a loathing for their Calvinist opinions.

His childhood was turbulent, with never-ceasing strife among his jealous nobility and between them and the politically active presbyterian clergy. Moray was murdered in 1570 and the king's grandfather, the Earl of Lennox, who became Regent in his place, was killed in a skirmish in 1571. Lord Mar succeeded Lennox as Regent and on his death in 1572 the office passed to the Earl of Morton who survived – with difficulty – until 1581, when he was executed – ostensibly for his complicity in the murder of the king's father, Darnley, in 1567. In August 1582 the king was seized by the Earl of Gowrie and fellow-plotters and held a virtual prisoner until he

REX ✠ SERENISSIMVS ORCAD IACOBVS SCOTORVM VI DEI GRATIA

QVOD SIS, ESSE VELIS.

Afra Iubam tellus, Cotyn effert Thracia, doctos
Reges: ingenium Scotica terra tuum.

9 E.374–1960

managed to escape in June 1583 to the protection of a group of nobles hostile to the Gowrie party. All James' experiences and instincts led him to the conclusion that he must strengthen the role of the crown to enable him to combat the arrogant pretensions of the nobility and the impertinences of the self-righteous clergy.

In the latter part of 1584 James and the Earl of Arran succeeded in defeating the Gowrie faction, forcing them to flee to England and. at the same time, he rid himself of the leader of the presbyterians, Andrew Melville, who also fled into England. Gowrie himself was captured and executed in May 1584.

The young king was clever and conceited, but timid and disinclined to devote himself to business. He was passionately fond of hunting and spent much of his time in this favourite pursuit. Obliged to choose between an alliance with France and the likelihood of greater influence for his virtually unknown mother, and one with England and the support of Elizabeth, he chose the latter, but not until Elizabeth, by inciting the Gowrie plotters to invade Scotland, had obliged him to disavow Arran, an ardent supporter of France and of Mary, who was obliged to flee. A treaty with England was finally concluded at Berwick on 2 July 1586. Mary felt obliged to 'disinherit' James and to 'bequeath' her former kingdom to Philip II of Spain (plate 2). The discovery of the Babington Plot soon followed and Mary was eventually executed in February 1587. James protested formally to Elizabeth about his mother's execution but bore it with equanimity, understanding clearly how an undisputed title to the throne of Scotland strengthened his case for succession to the English throne. He proceeded to improve his position by continuing his adherence to Elizabeth's interests and strongly supported the anti-Armada measures taken in Scotland in 1588. His mother's bequest of the Scottish crown to Spain undoubtedly strengthened his resolution to stand well with Elizabeth.

In 1589 James married Anne, the second daughter of Frederick III of Denmark (plate 10). In 1592 James agreed to an Act of Parliament establishing the presbyterian form of government in the Scottish Church, part of an attempt to strengthen his position by an alliance with the clergy against the nobility, whilst at the same time he was also attempting to reach an understanding with his Catholic nobles, led by the Earl of Huntly; the latter as a counter to the influence of the Protestant clergy, whose behaviour became increasingly intransigent and offensive to the king as his financial difficulties worsened.

In December 1596 James took the bold step of expelling from Edinburgh four ministers and 74 leading citizens and of removing himself and the courts of justice from the capital. This decisiveness worked and he was speedily able to return to the city in full control of the situation. In February 1597 he summoned an assembly of the clergy at Perth at which he was able to secure valuable concessions and to establish a useful constitutional relationship between himself and the kirk. In subsequent meetings inconclusive discussions took place on the representation of the clergy in Parliament. It was about this time that James began his writings on government and on the rights and duties of kings.

In August 1600 there occurred a sensational event which could have had the gravest consequences for James. He was seized at a house in Perth by Lord Gowrie (son of the earl executed in 1584) and his brother, Alexander Ruthven, who probably intended to murder him. The king, however, managed to attract the attention of his followers and the two brothers were killed and the king released.

In his impatience to obtain the succession to the English throne James now entered into many intrigues. He did not damage his cause, however, for Sir Robert Cecil, Elizabeth's secretary-of-state, was convinced that James must succeed, although the queen consistently refused to name her successor. Cecil accordingly kept in close touch with the king throughout the last years of Elizabeth's reign. On her deathbed the queen finally named James to succeed and on 24 March 1603 he was immediately proclaimed king in England. On 5 April he set out from Edinburgh on the the journey south to claim his English inheritance.

10 James I of England and VI of Scotland (1566–1625) with his consort Anne of Denmark (1574–1619)

From his accession to the English throne to his death

Engraving by Johan **Wierix**.

(O'D 78; Hind: Part II, p.57, 11, 1st state)

On coming into England James granted titles and lands with an unjustified prodigality prophetic of the extravagance which marked his reign. The king retained Robert Cecil (created Earl of Salisbury in 1605) as his principal adviser but weakened his council by removing from it men who disagreed with him. An early attempt was made to secure an immediate peace with Spain but this was not in fact achieved until 1604. Religious discontents surfaced almost immediately after the king's accession. He was initially sympathetic towards some relief for the Catholics from the severity of the recusancy laws and was, at the same time, prepared to listen to proposals from the Puritan clergy for some modification of the Anglican liturgy. However, the rapid increase in the number of priests and of Catholic converts in England and the personal irritation caused by the secret Catholic sympathies of his queen, Anne of Denmark, caused him to harden his attitude towards that minority, while his disputations with the dissenting clergy at the Hampton Court Conference in 1604 produced a similar reaction towards the Puritans. The English Parliament proved obstinate over the king's desired Act of Union with Scotland and was prorogued by him in July 1604. Those Puritan clergy who refused to conform were deprived of their livings and in February 1605 the king announced his determination fully to enforce the recusancy laws against the Catholics, a step which led directly to the Gunpowder Plot (plate 31).

James became increasingly unpopular despite his pacific intentions and his undoubted intellectual gifts. Prominent among the reasons for this were his arrogant intellectuality, his lack of personal charm, the unrebuked licence of his court and his favouritism towards Scotsmen in the distribution of awards and offices. His financial difficulties were such that he was prompted to serious discussion with

IACOBVS·ET·ANNA, REX·ET·REGINA·ANGLIÆ·FRANCIÆ·SCOTIÆ·ET·HIBERNIÆ.
IOHAN·WIRICX·F·ET·EXCVD·CVM·PRIVIL·SIG·DE·BVICHER·

Parliament about the possible surrender of his income from feudal dues in return for an annual fixed income. The proposal failed, however, and the first Parliament of the reign was dissolved in February 1611.

In foreign affairs the king attempted to exercise a moderating influence between the opposed Catholic and Protestant states. In 1611 he was engaged in abortive negotiations concerning a marriage between his eldest son (plate 11) and a Spanish princess and in March 1612 he entered into an alliance with the German Protestant princes during the negotiations for the marriage of his daughter Elizabeth (plate 12) to the Elector Palatine.

The death of Lord Salisbury in May 1612 deprived James of a moderating influence and a major source of cautious advice, while in November of the same year the Prince of Wales died (plate 11). The king's financial difficulties increased and he was obliged to summon another Parliament in 1614, but, disregarding popular opinion, he was unprepared to make any concessions on money matters or with regard to the expelled Puritan clergy and Parliament was dissolved in June having achieved nothing.

In this situation the king turned once again to Spain for support and a marriage between his son Charles and the Infanta Maria was discussed. A partially successful attempt to raise money was made through the imposition of greatly resented 'benevolences', or supposedly voluntary gifts to the king. James felt obliged to imprison some of the more outspoken opponents of his measures and his position was further weakened by the scandal surrounding the marriage of his favourite Robert Carr, Earl of Somerset, to Frances Howard, Countess of Essex, and their subsequent trial and conviction for the murder of Sir Thomas Overbury in 1616. In that same year James at last succeeded in dismissing the independent-minded Lord Chief Justice, Sir Edward Coke, whom he had long disliked as an enemy of the royal prerogative.

In 1617 steps were taken to open formal negotiations for the marriage of Prince Charles to the Infanta Maria. This was very unpopular as was the king's foolish fondness for his new favourite, George Villiers, newly-created Earl of Buckingham. Also in 1617 James undertook a journey into Scotland which he used to attempt to achieve – with some success – greater conformity to Anglican rites and practices in the Scottish Church.

The year 1618 saw the failure of the last voyage of Sir Walter Ralegh (plate 34) to Guiana and James had no compunction in allowing the execution of this arch-enemy of Spain in accordance with the sentence awarded in 1603 for Ralegh's involvement in Lord Cobham's plot. James's Spanish policy was now complicated by the outbreak of what was to develop into the Thirty Years' War and the threat to his family interest in the fate of the Palatinate, although James continued to see himself as a mediator, a reconciler of opposing interests and a force for peace in Europe.

In March 1619 the amiable, pleasure-loving queen died from dropsy after a long and painful illness. During her years in England Queen Anne had been much concerned with the arts, especially with masquing and architecture, both interests being reflected pre-eminently in her patronage of Inigo Jones. She was responsible for much of the extravagant royal expenditure on entertainments which went hand in hand with her husband's excessive generosity

to his friends and favourites. However, during her last years there had been some degree of estrangement from the king, largely due to her Catholic propensities.

Throughout 1620 James's policy vacillated between placating Spain and offering some support and encouragement to the allies of his son-in-law, Frederick of the Palatinate. His irresolution was such that he allowed himself to be swayed by whichever ambassador was currently pleading his cause. In order to raise money James again summoned Parliament in January 1621. Although distrustful of the king's intentions it voted funds to provide military assistance to the Palatinate and went on to discuss financial corruption, proceedings which eventually led to the disgrace of Francis Bacon, the Lord Chancellor (plate 30). In December 1621 the Commons petitioned the king, asking him to assume leadership of the Protestant states, to suppress the Catholic recusants at home and to arrange a Protestant marriage for Prince Charles. The king refused to accept the Commons' recommendations and adjourned Parliament, finally dissolving it in January 1622. As no money had been voted James was obliged to raise funds through further 'benevolences' and similar impositions.

The war in Europe continued to go badly, so that eventually all the Palatinate had to be surrendered to the victorious Catholic forces. James still vainly hoped to restore the balance through the good offices of Spain, but Spain was quite unable to act against fellow Catholic powers and while marriage negotiations continued with Spain throughout 1622 the military situation in the Palatinate went from bad to worse. In January 1623 James and Charles signed the marriage agreement but very soon

after this Charles and Buckingham resolved to go to Spain to test for themselves the Spanish intentions in the matter. Their visit, lasting several months, made clear the impossibility of proceeding with the Spanish match on terms of any real advantage to England. Soon after their return Parliament met again in February 1624 and petitioned for the abandonment of the negotiations. This received reluctant agreement from the king late in March.

From that date until his death James effectively ceased to rule, power passing into the hands of the Prince of Wales and Buckingham (by now created a duke). Fresh negotiations were begun for the marriage of the prince to Henrietta Maria, sister of Louis XIII of France, a treaty being signed in November 1624. An attempt by James to secure a military intervention in the Palatinate came to nothing for lack of funds.

Early in March 1625 the king fell ill with a fever which failed to respond to treatment and he died at Theobalds on 27 March. He was buried in Westminster Abbey on 5 May 1625.

11 Henry Frederick, Prince of Wales (1594–1612)

Engraving by William **Hole**. Frontispiece to *Polyolbion* by Michael Drayton, published by M Lownes, London, 1612. After a lost miniature by Isaac **Oliver**.

(O'D 16, 1st state; Hind: Part II, p.321, 9, 1st state; R S, p.164)

Henry Frederick, Prince of Wales, was the

11   E.1580–1960

eldest son of James VI of Scotland and I of England by his wife Anne of Denmark (plate 10). He was born at Stirling Castle on 19 February 1594, his birth causing great rejoicing throughout Scotland. Early in 1595 he was confided to the guardianship of the Earl of Mar, with special responsibility for his well-being falling upon the Dowager Lady Mar who had charge of the prince's father during his infancy. The king wished the prince to remain with the Mars until he reached the age of 18 but this intention was changed on James's accession to the English throne in 1603, for Anne of Denmark refused to leave Scotland without her son.

Soon after his arrival in England in June 1603 the prince was invested with the Order of the Garter at Windsor and subsequently took up residence at Oatlands in Surrey, with occasional visits to Hampton Court. Proposals were under consideration between 1604 and 1607 for his engagement to the Infanta Anna of Spain but nothing came of them. In August 1605 the Prince matriculated at Magdalen College, Oxford, but it is clear that he was fonder of horsemanship, the sports of the tilt-yard and military and naval matters than he was of academic pursuits, despite his later considerable patronage of the arts. Among his closest friends was Sir Walter Ralegh (plate 34) who began to write his *History of the World* for the prince and for whom the prince did his best to secure his release from the Tower.

In June 1610 Henry was created Prince of Wales and was permitted to establish his own court at St James's Palace, which became much more frequented than the court of his father at Whitehall. The architect and designer Inigo Jones was appointed surveyor to the prince at this time, although French and Italian designers were also employed by him, especially on his gardens at Richmond. Henry, like his mother, was devoted to masquing and commissioned Jones and the playwright Ben Jonson to produce a series of chivalric entertainments in which he took the principal part.

However, all this bright promise was cruelly ended by Henry's death from typhoid fever on 6 November 1612, leaving his ill-fated brother, Charles, Duke of York, as heir to the throne. Henry was buried in Westminster Abbey on 8 November amidst universal mourning, for he was a gifted and popular prince. He was described some 30 years after his death as having been 'of a comely, tall, middle stature, about five feet and eight inches high, of a strong, straight, well-made body (as if Nature in him had shewed all her cunning) with somewhat broad shoulders, and a small waist, of an amiable Majestick Coutenance, his hair of an Auborne Collour, long faced and broad forehead, a piercing, grave eye, a most gracious smile with a terrible frowne, courteous, loving'.

This engraving by William Hole, based on a large miniature by Isaac Oliver, which was at one time in the royal collection and subsequently lost, shows the prince exercising with the pike.

12 Elizabeth, Princess Royal, Queen of Bohemia, Electress Palatine (1596–1662)

Daughter of James I; 'The Winter Queen' and 'Queen of Hearts'

Engraving by Boëtius Adams **Bolswert** after a painting by Michiel Jansz. **Miereveld.**

(O'D 11)

The Princess Elizabeth, eldest daughter of James VI of Scotland (later James I of England) and his consort Anne of Denmark (plate 10), was born at Falkland Castle in Fife in August 1596 and spent the first years of her childhood at Linlithgow Palace. In June 1603, soon after her father's accession to the throne of England, she travelled into England with her mother and from October 1603 to the end of 1608 she was under the kind and careful guardianship of Lord and Lady Harington at Combe Abbey in Warwickshire. While she was there the Gunpowder Plot conspirators (plate 31) determined, if all went well with their plot, to kidnap her on the day of the planned explosion at Westminster. In the event the attempt was never made.

From the end of 1608 she spent much time at court where she appeared in masques and began to attract great attention by her beauty. Various suggestions for royal marriages were made, including one from Spain and another from Sweden. In 1612, however, her father James I concluded a treaty of alliance with the German Protestant princes and in May of that year a marriage was arranged between Elizabeth and the handsome young Elector, Frederick V of the Palatinate, the leader of the princes. The couple were, fortunately, attracted to each other but Elizabeth's happiness was gravely marred by the death of her greatly beloved brother Henry, Prince of Wales (plate II) on 6 November. The wedding, however, went ahead as planned, taking place on 14 February 1613. In April the young couple set sail for Germany, eventually making their entry into Heidelberg on 17 June. Their extravagant mode of life occasioned much surprise and comment; their love, however, was sincere and deep. Their first child, Prince Frederick Henry, was born on 2 January 1614.

On the death of the Emperor Matthias in 1619 the Bohemians chose the Elector-Palatine as their king in preference to the previously elected Catholic Archduke Ferdinand of Styria. The latter was immediately elected as the new Emperor, with the title of Ferdinand II, and speedily began his campaign of revenge against the King of Bohemia. The couple arrived in Prague on 31 October 1619 and were crowned there almost at once. They were not popular, however, because of the queen's apparent levity and love of entertainment and their supposedly extreme Protestantism. The Emperor's troops attacked in Bohemia and on 8 November 1620 at the Battle of the White Hill, near Prague, Frederick's army was totally defeated and his short reign was effectively at an end. It was this brevity of the reign which caused him to be popularly known as 'The Winter King'. Soon his own territories in the Palatinate were overrun by Spanish and Bavarian troops and in this extremity both the king and his consort showed great calmness and courage. They were at last obliged to flee into Brandenburg where their children found refuge in Berlin;

they then travelled on into exile in the Netherlands where they arrived in April 1621. Within a very short time Frederick found himself deprived of his Electorate, the Palatinate being granted instead to the Duke of Bavaria at the conference of princes held at Ratisbon (or Regensburg) in 1622–23.

Eventually Frederick and Elizabeth settled down to a life of exile in a country house at Rhenen, near Arnhem, on the Rhine, living with their ever-increasing family as best they could on a grant from the States-General of the Netherlands and irregular cash contributions sent by Elizabeth's brother Charles I of England. Elizabeth remained cheerful and in good spirits, indulging her taste for hunting and regular riding. In 1629 their eldest son was drowned and there was a further blow in 1631 when another of their children, aged only three, also died. Their hopes of restoration were raised, however, in the years 1631–32 with the military successes in Germany of the Protestant King Gustavus Adolphus of Sweden, but in November 1632 Gustavus was killed at the Battle of Lützen and a few days later, on 29 November, Frederick himself died at Mainz.

For the next 16 years of her widowhood Elizabeth devoted herself to the interests of the survivors of her 13 children, although she does not seem to have extended any great affection to them – with the notable exception of her favourite son Prince Rupert who was soon to earn fame in the battles of the English Civil War. Her brother Charles I invited her to England but she declined, preferring to stay in Holland where she and her eldest surviving son Charles struggled on in vain efforts to recover their lost lands. It was not until the Peace of Westphalia of 1648 that a part of

their territories, the lands of the Rhenish Palatinate, were restored to her son. During these years the States-General of the Netherlands continued to pay Elizabeth the allowance made by them to her late husband. The intermittent aid from England ceased under the pressure of the Civil War and Elizabeth's means became increasingly straitened. The queen had, however, the power of inspiring great devotion in her many friends and among these the ever-loyal Earl of Craven continued to contribute whatever he could to her finances. Elizabeth's son Charles after his restoration, however, showed considerable coolness towards his mother and contributed virtually nothing to her expenses; in fairness it should be said in excuse of this latter apparent meanness that his lands had been totally devastated during the course of the wars of religion.

Elizabeth was greatly distressed by the execution of Charles I in January 1649 and that event, of course, put an end to any thoughts she may have had of returning to England after her son's failure to invite her back to the Palatinate. She remained in Holland dependent on the generosity of the Dutch and in touch with the exiled court of her nephew Charles II.

At Charles' restoration in 1660 she expected to travel to England immediately, but there was a tedious delay while attempts were made to resolve the problems posed by her debts and there was long delay in payment. Although uninvited she resolved to attend Charles' coronation and arrived in London about the end of May 1661. Early in February 1662 she moved into a London residence of her own, Leicester House in Leicester Fields, but died there only a week later on 13 February. Four days later she was buried in Westminster Abbey.

Elizabeth was clearly a woman of great personal charm and considerable energy and spirit, capable of inspiring lasting loyalty among those devoted to her cause. As a girl she attracted many tributes to her beauty and charm, but when Pepys met her in The Hague on 17 May 1660 he thought her by then to be 'a very debonaire, but plain lady'.

The engraving, dated 1615, shows Elizabeth at the age of 16 in 1613. A companion portrait of her husband of the same date was also engraved by B A Bolswert after Miereveld.

13 **William Cecil, 1st Baron Burghley, KG (1520–1598)**

Statesman; Lord High Treasurer, 1572–1598

Engraving possibly by William **Rogers,** probably after a portrait by Marcus **Gheeraerts II.**

(O'D 9; Hind: Part I, pp.261–262, 3; R S, p.32 and plate 57)

William Cecil, better known under his later title of Lord Burghley, was a loyal servant to the three children of Henry VIII during their successive reigns, but it is his long and faithful service to Elizabeth I which gives him a unique place in history for he was senior adviser to the queen for no less than 40 years. He was the only son of Richard Cecil, a wealthy Northamptonshire squire formerly in the service of Henry VIII. Educated at the grammar schools of Stamford and Grantham he went

13 E.3315–1960

on to become a good Greek scholar at St John's College, Cambridge. He fell in love with the penniless sister of his fellow-scholar John Cheke and, as a result, was removed from Cambridge by his father and entered at Gray's Inn in 1541. Nevertheless, he subsequently married Mary Cheke and his son Thomas was born in 1542. His wife, however, died in 1544.

Cecil prepared to make his career as a lawyer and in 1547 he obtained a lucrative office in the Court of Common Pleas. He remarried in 1545, his bride being Mildred, the daughter of Sir Anthony Cooke, preceptor to the young Prince Edward. On Edward's accession to the throne early in 1547 Cecil was made Master of Requests by Lord Protector Somerset and represented Stamford in the Parliament. In 1548 he became Somerset's secretary and was committed to the Tower when the Lord Protector fell from power in 1549. His stay there was short, however, and he was appointed one of the secretaries of state and sworn a member of the Privy Council in September 1550. From this date until his death – virtually without a break – he remained in royal service, eventually becoming on Queen Elizabeth's accession the most influential minister in the kingdom. His great wisdom, loyalty and capacity for business made him virtually indispensable to government. He was knighted in 1551 and inherited his father's large estate in May 1552. He resigned his secretaryship in 1553, at the time of Northumberland's attempt to set Lady Jane Grey on the throne at the death of Edward VI, and turned his energies towards the building of his great houses at Burghley and Wimbledon. Mary 1 (plate 1), however, chose to send him on a mission in November 1554 to bring Cardinal Pole to

England as Papal Legate and he continued to serve Mary as a diplomatist and had a seat in the Parliament of 1557. By 1558, however, it seemed likely that the queen would soon die and Cecil entered into discreet discussions with the Princess Elizabeth so that on Mary's death on 17 November 1558 he was fully in the confidence of the new queen who at once made him her chief secretary of state, saying to him, 'This judgement I have of you, that you will not be corrupted with any manner of gifts, and that you will be faithful to the state'. As the queen's faithful principal servant the remaining 40 years of his astonishing career are virtually identified with the history of England during Elizabeth's reign. As a statesman he was subtle and cautious, committed to maintaining his sovereign on her throne and the Protestant ascendancy in England. As a private person he was kind and charitable but, fully understanding the strength of Catholic feeling in the country and the political threat inherent in the excommunication of the queen in 1570, he reacted with uncharacteristic harshness to the recusants, the Catholic missionaries and their followers.

The organization of the queen's intelligence service was a major contribution made by Burghley to the security of the realm. Its efficiency was unparalleled and undoubtedly enabled Elizabeth to pursue a highly sophisticated diplomatic policy as well as securing her from the menace of her enemies active in England.

In 1559 Cecil became Chancellor of the University of Cambridge. In 1561 he was granted the very lucrative office of Master of the Court of Wards. In 1571 he was created Baron Burghley and in 1572 he was made a Knight of the Garter and Lord High Treasurer,

an office which he held until his death at Burghley House in the Strand on 4 August 1598. He is buried in St Martin's Church, Stamford. He is said to have been of medium height and spare figure but distinguished by the brilliancy of his eyes.

The portrait from which this engraving derives probably dates from the mid-1580s and, therefore, shows Burghley as he appeared in his mid-60s.

14 E.3850-1960

14 Robert Dudley, 1st Earl of Leicester, KG (1532?–1588)

Master of the Horse; favourite of Queen Elizabeth

Engraving by Hieronymus **Wierix**.

(O'D 14)

Robert Dudley, the fifth son of John Dudley, 1st Duke of Northumberland, by his wife Jane Guilford, was born on 23 June 1532 or 1533. He was well educated privately and when aged about 16 was introduced by his father into the company of the young King Edward and his half-sister the Princess Elizabeth, later to be queen. She was of his own age and was apparently attracted from the first by his handsome person. However, on 4 June 1550 he married Amy, daughter of Sir John Robsart of Norfolk, and after the marriage the couple lived for some years in Norfolk, Dudley being MP for the county in 1553. He made appearances at court, nevertheless, and received various minor appointments from the king.

On the death of the king in July 1553 Dudley was involved with his father and brothers in the abortive plot to place Lady Jane Grey on the throne. He was sentenced to death by Queen Mary I (plate 1) for his part in the conspiracy but was eventually pardoned. In 1557 he accompanied two of his brothers to France with the English army and as a result of his services he appears to have found some favour with King Philip (plate 2).

On Queen Elizabeth's accession in 1558 Dudley seized the opportunity presented by his old friendship and quickly ingratiated himself with the new queen. He was appointed Master of the Horse in January 1559, created Knight of the Garter in April and soon afterwards was appointed to the Privy Council.

In November, after a great success in a tournament at Greenwich, he received gifts of lands and financial privileges from the queen. It is clear that she was infatuated and was seriously considering the possibility of marriage. In the meantime Dudley's wife was living a somewhat nomadic life in the country, but he continued to visit her and they remained on good terms. Early in 1560 his wife went to live at Cumnor Place in Oxfordshire and it was there that she met her death on 8 September, falling down a flight of stairs in circumstances which gave rise to suspicions of both murder and suicide. It was supposed that she had either been killed, so that her husband would be free to marry the queen, or that she had killed herself in despair at the supposed liaison. No conclusive evidence was discovered to support either theory and the coroner's jury brought in a verdict of accidental death.

The affair caused much adverse speculation, gossip declaring that Dudley had spoken of either divorcing or poisoning his wife many months before her death. The rumours of murder were, of course, carefully propagated by those at court determined to prevent at all costs a marriage between Dudley and the queen. Negotiations were begun by the queen and Dudley with the Spanish ambassador to explore the possibility of such a marriage receiving Spanish support in exchange for an undertaking to restore Roman Catholicism in England.

By 1563, however, the queen apparently had reached the conclusion that marriage with Dudley was impossible. She was frequently angered by his presumption and became increasingly aware of the threat to her own position that such a marriage would constitute. Soon she was even suggesting a marriage between Dudley and Mary, Queen of Scots (plate 6). In mid-1564 Dudley was known to be still attempting to ingratiate himself with Spain, and in September of that year he was created Earl of Leicester. This advancement was intended to further the proposed match with Mary, but all hopes in this direction were ended by Mary's marriage to the young Lord Darnley (plate 8) in July 1565.

In 1566 Leicester's position was threatened by a renewed proposal of marriage made to Elizabeth by the Archduke Charles of Austria. He did his best to wreck the negotiations and deserted the Spanish and Catholic party, offering his support to the Puritans instead. Opposition to the proposed match was considerable and by 1568 the idea had been abandoned. Once the threat was removed Leicester received further gifts of land and privileges from the queen. He then proceeded to intrigue against Cecil, abetted the Catholic lords who were considering rebellion, entered into negotiations with the exiled Mary Stuart to forward the Catholic plan for a marriage between her and the Duke of Norfolk and generally sought to protect his own position should that of the queen be threatened. Despite his base behaviour he still remained in favour with the queen, even after the imprisonment of Norfolk and the defeat of the rebellion of the northern earls at the close of 1569.

In 1570–71 he strongly supported the proposal for a marriage between Elizabeth and the French prince the Duke of Anjou. In 1571 he himself was deeply involved in an intrigue with the widowed Lady Sheffield and in May 1573 he married her, the marriage being kept secret from the queen so that Leicester's position at court should not be endangered.

In July 1575 he entertained the queen lavishly at Kenilworth Castle and in September 1577 he sought for himself the post of commander-in-chief of the army which the queen was contemplating sending against the Spanish forces in the Netherlands. This came to nothing, however, much to Leicester's disappointment. Early in 1578 the Duke of Alençon renewed his proposal for marriage with Elizabeth, the approach being received seriously. Leicester, by now tired of his new – but unacknowledged – wife was in active pursuit of Lady Essex, widow of the 1st Earl of Essex, and with the renewal of Alençon's proposal he abandoned all hope of marrying the queen. In September 1578 he married Lady Essex, the marriage being publicly celebrated and known to many at court although carefully concealed from the queen. In August 1579 the news was deliberately broken to her by the French ambassador and Elizabeth appeared to be heartbroken, threatening Leicester with imprisonment in the Tower. On this occasion, however, she made a speedy recovery from her anger and he was soon permitted to return to court.

Leicester having assisted in ensuring that the new French marriage proposal failed, began to envisage a new role for himself. This was as the possible leader and prince of the Protestant provinces of the Netherlands. His pride and ambition were at their height and there was now a general hatred directed against him. A scurrilous pamphlet in English was published in Antwerp in 1584 accusing him of the murder of Amy Robsart and many other crimes. He formulated ambitious plans for the marriage of his infant son to Lady Arabella Stuart (a possible claimant to the throne on Elizabeth's death) and for the marriage of one of his step-daughters to James VI of Scotland. Late in 1584, at a time of considerable unrest among the Catholic nobility and gentry, Leicester suggested the formation of the celebrated Association for the protection of the queen and the succession.

In the autumn of 1585 Elizabeth finally appointed Leicester to command an English expedition to fight against Spain in the Netherlands. He made a triumphal progress through the provinces and in January 1586 was offered the absolute government of the United Provinces, which he accepted after some protestation. Elizabeth was furious, threatened his recall and despite the political arguments of Burghley and other counsellors could not be brought to relent until the Dutch themselves petitioned her to do so. Leicester, however, proved to be an incompetent commander and behaved arrogantly towards the Dutch. His campaign was lethargic and proved to be inconclusive. He returned to England at the end of 1586 and did all that he could to persuade Elizabeth to agree to the execution of Mary Stuart. The Dutch asked for his return and the queen finally permitted him to go. The English army, however, was in wretched condition and so demoralized that nothing could be achieved and in April 1588 he finally resigned his office as governor.

On returning home he was made 'lieutenant and captain-general of the queen's armies and companies'. He was at the camp at Tilbury during the period of possible invasion by the Armada and with the queen at her review of the troops in August after its defeat. At the end of August he left London for Kenilworth but died on his journey, at his house at Cornbury in Oxfordshire. Rumour had it that he had been poisoned, either by his wife unknowingly administering a poisoned cordial intended by her husband for herself or through her premeditation to enable her to marry Blount, which she did soon after Leicester's death.

Rumours of poisoning had been with Leicester throughout his life. Poison had been mentioned as the originally intended method of removing Amy Robsart and he was also said to have poisoned both Lord Sheffield and Lord Essex in order to obtain their wives. There is, however, no real evidence to prove the truth of any of these assertions. They do serve, nevertheless, to demonstrate the general hatred and contempt which was felt for Leicester.

His pride, ambition, vanity, misuse of women and the general baseness of character evidenced by his calculated dealings with the Catholic and Protestant parties in turn are sufficient grounds to justify such an opinion. He was essentially a man of little worth who owed everything to his handsome person and his continuing influence with the queen.

The engraving appears to date from about 1586 and was probably prompted by Leicester's role as commander of the forces in the Netherlands. Like other head and shoulders portraits of this type it may derive from a full-length portrait of that date by an unidentified artist which is at Parham Park in Sussex.

The Right Honourable Charles Howard Earle of
Nottingham, Baron of Effinghā, Lord high Admirall
of England and Ireland. Chiefe Iustice in Ere over
all his Ma:ties fforests Parks and Chases on this side Trent
Knight of the most noble order of the Garter, and one of his Ma:ties
most honorable privy counsell.

Si Passeus sculp: most honorable Compton Holland excud:

15   E.3111–1960

15   Charles Howard, 1st Earl of Nottingham, 2nd Baron Howard of Effingham, KG (1536–1624)

Lord High Admiral

Engraving by Simon van de **Passe** after a painting of *c* 1600 known from versions at Hampton Court and Knole.

(O'D 12; Hind: Part II, p.263, 41; R S, p.236)

Charles Howard (best known to posterity by his subsidiary title of Lord Howard of Effingham) was the eldest son of William, 1st Baron Howard of Effingham and a grandson of the Duke of Norfolk. He was also cousin to the queen through her grandmother Elizabeth Howard, daughter of the Duke of Norfolk, a relationship which undoubtedly contributed to his advancement. His father had been Lord Admiral and later Lord Chamberlain to Queen Mary I and was again Lord Chamberlain to Queen Elizabeth. Whilst serving as Lord Admiral Howard's father became popular with his seamen and it seems likely that as a sailor himself he would have encouraged his son to gain the active experience at sea which later stood him in such good stead.

Soon after Elizabeth's accession Howard served as ambassador to France and was MP for Surrey in the Parliament of 1562. In 1569 he served as a general in the campaign against the northern rebels and in 1570 he was in command of a squadron of warships sent to escort the Queen of Spain on her passage from Flanders through the English Channel and it is supposed that he was knighted about this time. He again represented Surrey in the Parliament of 1572 and early in the following year succeeded to his father's title. In April 1574 he became a Knight of the Garter and soon afterwards was appointed Lord Chamberlain, an office which he held until 1585 when he became Lord High Admiral. In 1586 he served as a commissioner for the trial of Mary, Queen of Scots (plate 7), and is believed to have been largely responsible for finally convincing the reluctant Queen Elizabeth that she had no alternative to signing Mary's death-warrant.

In December 1587 Howard was granted a special commission as commander-in-chief of both the navy and the army then being prepared to go to sea against Spain with Sir Francis Drake (plate 33) as his second-in-command. The prudent harrying tactics used by the English fleet against the Armada in 1588 seem to have been decided largely by Howard, aware of his own deficiencies in men and in the weight and power of his ships. He customarily consulted fully with his council of war, drawn from the commanders within his fleet, before commencing any major tactic. That he was a careful and conscientious commander much concerned for the welfare of his men is shown by the relief measures he took when many of his seamen fell ill, due to bad provisions, after the final successful action against the Spaniards off Gravelines. He put a large number of men ashore at Margate and made himself personally responsible for procuring adequate shelter and provisions for them at his own expense, the queen's parsimony being so great that even at that auspicious time she demurred at the extra cost involved.

After the defeat of the Armada Howard was kept at home by the claims of his high office in the administration of the navy and the defence of the kingdom, but in 1596 another attempt to invade England was in preparation by the Spaniards and a fleet and an army under the joint command of Howard and the Earl of Essex (plate 18) were put in readiness. The fleet, consisting of 17 warships with supporting transports, arrived off Cadiz on 20 June and on the following day the Spanish ships in the port were defeated with many destroyed and two captured. Other vessels about to sail with valuable cargoes were destroyed by their crews instead of being captured, for Essex had impetuously decided to land as soon as the Spanish ships gave way. Howard was obliged to land in support and the town was eventually sacked and destroyed and the forts dismantled. After the action no less than 66 knighthoods were conferred on individual commanders by the generals. Howard's caution and his unwillingness to take unnecessary risks were again in evidence, for having achieved the principal aim of the expedition, which was the destruction of shipping, he returned to England without further pillaging expeditions. The queen, while agreeing with the tactics, showed some disappointment at the absence of captured treasure.

In the following year Howard was created Earl of Nottingham, his patent of nobility referring not only to his services against the Armada but also to his achievements at Cadiz. This roused the jealous anger of Essex who wished to claim all credit for the success of the Cadiz expedition and soured relations between the two men even further. However, Elizabeth's trust in Nottingham continued to be great and is well demonstrated by his unprecedented appointment in 1599, during a period of extreme alarm at supposed renewed Spanish invasion threats, as Lord Lieutenant-General of all England, an office of supreme authority which he held for six weeks until the threat was seen to be without real basis.

At Essex's trial for treason in 1601 Nottingham was one of the commissioners and, after the earl's execution, served on the commission appointed to perform the duties of Essex's late office of Earl Marshal. He remained in high favour and was in attendance at the queen's death-bed, it being to him that she named James VI of Scotland as her successor. Nottingham was in close communication with the new king from the outset of his reign and was at once confirmed in his office of Lord Admiral and continued to be nominated to undertake arduous and responsible duties. In March 1605 he went to Spain as ambassador to conclude the peace negotiated with that country by the king. He was attended in the most magnificent style and behaved with great courtliness and liberality. His reputation as a successful commander, joined to his firmness, courtesy and good temper, made a great impression on the Spaniards and contributed greatly to the success of his mission. The years following saw his official involvement in all major affairs of state. At the marriage of Princess Elizabeth (plate 12), the king's daughter, to the Elector Palatine in 1613 the princess was attended by Nottingham and the Duke of Lennox and his last naval service was to command the squadron which escorted her to Flushing. In 1619, after the report of a commission enquiring into certain abuses in the administration of the navy, Nottingham chose to resign his office as Lord Admiral, although the commission in no way censured him.

He continued to serve as Lord-Lieutenant of Surrey and to hold various royal appointments which provided a substantial income. He remained generous in his dealings and seems at no time to have been blamed for corruption or avarice. He died at his house at Haling, near Croydon, on 14 December 1624 and was buried in the family vault in Reigate Church. He was married twice, first to Catherine, daughter of Lord Hunsdon, who died in February 1603, and secondly, in 1604, to Lady Margaret Stuart, daughter of the Earl of Moray. By his first marriage he had two sons and three daughters, and by the second he had two sons.

This portrait, dating from about 1600, shows Nottingham when in his mid-60s.

16 E.3122–1960

16 Edward Somerset, 4th Earl of Worcester, KG (c 1550–1628)

Statesman and courtier

Engraving by Simon van de **Passe** after a portrait by an unidentified artist.

(O'D 3; Hind: Part II, p.270, 57, 1st state)

Edward Somerset was the only son of William Somerset, 3rd Earl of Worcester, by his wife Christian, daughter of the 1st Baron North. He achieved fame in his youth for his skill as a horseman and in the tiltyard and, despite his constant adherence to the Roman Catholic faith, he became a favourite with the queen. In December 1571 he married Elizabeth Hastings, daughter of the 2nd Earl of Huntingdon, and by that marriage had five sons and seven daughters. He succeeded his father in 1589 and in 1590 was sent by the queen as ambassador to Scotland to congratulate James VI on his marriage to Anne of Denmark (plate 10) and to invest the king with the insignia of the Order of the Garter. He was made a councillor of Wales in the same year and was himself given the Garter in April 1593.

He became Deputy-Master of the Horse in 1597 and in 1600 was appointed a member of the court set up to hear the charges against the Earl of Essex (plate 18). He was subsequently detained by Essex along with other notables on 8 February 1601 when they came to Essex House in London to enquire into the reasons for the suspicious assembly there. Whilst he held prisoner these high officers of state Essex attempted to raise the population of London in his support but failed to achieve the favourable response he had expected. He was subsequently tried and condemned by a court of peers which included Worcester.

After the execution of Essex Worcester was made Master of the Horse in his place and later in 1601 he was appointed to the Privy Council and became a joint-commissioner for the office of Earl Marshal formerly held by Essex. In 1602 he was appointed Lord-Lieutenant of Monmouthshire and Glamorganshire.

Worcester continued in royal favour after the accession of James I in 1603 and served as Earl Marshal at his coronation and on subsequent occasions until 1617. In 1604, despite his Catholicism, he served on a commission to consider the expulsion of the Jesuits and was one of those who examined the captured Gunpowder Plot conspirators (plate 31). On Lord Salisbury's death he was appointed Lord Privy Seal in January 1616. He was one of the commissioners who examined Ralegh in 1618 and in February 1621 he became a Judge of Requests. The last great office he held was that of Lord Great Chamberlain at the coronation of Charles I in 1626.

He died on 3 March 1628 at Worcester House in the Strand 'aged about 79' and was buried at Raglan, his principal seat. His career demonstrates how a staunch Roman Catholic could achieve high office and hold posts of great responsibility under the crown in the reigns of both Elizabeth and James, providing that his loyalty to the sovereign and to the state were known to be unequivocal.

This engraved portrait, dated 1618, shows the earl in old age and at the height of his prestige and influence and is taken from a painting at Gorhambury, near St Albans, Hertfordshire.

The right Honorable GEORGE Earle of Cumber: land, Lo: Clifford of Skipton, Knight of the most noble Ordre of the Garter and one of her M^{ties} most Honorable privy Counsell

Are to be sold by Compton Holland over against the Exchange

17 E.3651-1960

17 George Clifford, 3rd Earl of Cumberland, KG (1558–1605)

Naval Commander

Engraving by Robert **Vaughan** after an unidentified painting.

(O'D 8; C and N 14, 2nd state; R S, p.58, plate 102)

George Clifford was born at Brougham Castle in Westmorland on 8 August 1558, the son of the 2nd Earl of Cumberland by his second wife Anne, daughter of Lord Dacre. He succeeded to the title on his father's death in 1570 and became the ward of the Earl of Bedford, spending the later part of his childhood at either Chenies in Buckinghamshire or at Woburn. He entered Trinity College, Cambridge, in 1571 and was in residence until 1574, becoming MA in November 1576. He is said to have had a special proficiency in mathematics and a great interest in geography.

In June 1577 he married Lady Margaret Russell, the daughter of his guardian, a marriage which had been arranged in the infancy of both. It turned out, however, to be an unhappy union and ended in separation many years later. Cumberland proved to be a spendthrift, a gambler and highly attractive to women. Much of his inheritance was wasted on his pleasures and he therefore welcomed the opportunity to attempt to restore his depleted fortunes which was offered by the war with Spain. The result, over the years, was that he became financially involved with

no less than 10 expeditions which caused him great expense but, generally speaking, produced little profit for him.

His first involvement occurred in 1586 when he fitted out a small force which sailed to the River Plate under the command of Captain Widrington but failed to take any prizes or secure any booty. He was appointed a member of the commission for the execution of Mary Stuart in 1587 and in 1588 was given command of one of the queen's ships sailing against the Armada. After the decisive action off Gravelines he personally carried the news of the victory back to the camp at Tilbury. His conduct greatly pleased the queen and later in 1588 she assisted him in fitting out another small fleet commanded by himself, but again this force, because of bad weather, had no success in its quest for prizes. However, the queen once more gave some assistance in 1589 towards assembling a fleet of seven ships which sailed from Plymouth in mid-June. This force did succeed in seizing many enemy ships in the Channel, off Portugal and in the Azores, eventually seizing the richest prize of all, from the Spanish West Indies fleet, valued at £100,000. Further prizes were taken and Cumberland was badly wounded in the course of one of these actions. When at last the fleet was ready to sail for home it found itself overburdened with prizes and prisoners. The rich West Indiaman became a total loss in Mount's Bay and the fleet became desperately short of water. The earl behaved with great equanimity in this time of stress and finally managed to obtain from a passing English vessel sufficient relief to get his vessels to Ireland and eventually into Falmouth at the very end of the year. However, this expedition seemed to establish a pattern of misfortune which was to afflict Cumberland in his future maritime enterprises.

He financed annual expeditions from 1591 to 1596, sometimes under his own command and sometimes commanded by officers of his choice. The overall record of these enterprises was, however, extremely disappointing to the earl who seems to have been dogged by ill-luck, manifested in bad weather, loss of prizes, sickness and other misfortunes.

In 1590 Cumberland had been appointed the queen's Champion and in June 1592, during a period of close attendance on the queen at court and her progresses, he was created a Knight of the Garter. He eventually became a member of the Privy Council under the new king in 1603.

In 1598 he undertook his largest maritime venture in assuming financial responsibility for 20 ships which sailed from Plymouth, under his personal command, to the Canaries, Dominica and Puerto Rico, where they intended to expel the Spaniards from San Juan and establish an English colony in its place. Misfortune struck once again, however, and sickness among the troops prevented this project from being pursued, with the result that the expedition finally returned home empty-handed.

Cumberland died at Duchy House, Middlesex, on 29 October 1605 and was buried in the family vault at Skipton in Yorkshire. He was clearly a man of great personal courage as well as being an accomplished courtier. His career seems to have been something of a failure, possibly due in part to his rashness and over-optimism. He is known to have been handsome and a popular romantic figure but was, unfortunately, an inveterate gambler who damaged his reputation further by his indulgence in 'low amours'.

The portrait shows the earl as he appeared about 1590 and was probably engraved by Robert Vaughan from a painting similar to one which still survives at Knole House, near Sevenoaks, Kent.

18 Robert Devereux, 2nd Earl of Essex, KG (1566–1601)

Military commander and courtier

Engraving by William **Rogers,** probably after a portrait by Marcus **Gheerhaerts II**.

(O'D 19; Hind: Part I, p.267, 10, after 2nd state; R S, p.116)

Robert Devereux, the eldest son of Walter Devereux, 1st Earl of Essex, by his wife Lettice Knollys, was born 19 November 1566 at Netherwood in Herefordshire. On the death of his father in 1576 he inherited the impoverished family estates and was made a ward of Lord Burghley (plate 13). In May 1576 he entered Trinity College, Cambridge, being created MA in July 1581.

At Christmas 1577 he made his first appearance at court but after leaving Cambridge he appears to have spent some years quietly on his estates. In 1584 he reappeared at court where his handsome person and good manner brought him notice. In August 1585 he accompanied his stepfather, the Earl of Leicester (plate 14), on the expedition to the Low Countries and served with distinction at the Battle of Zutphen. He was at court in 1587 and received considerable attention from the queen. In December 1587 he was appointed Master of the Horse and in April 1588 was made a Knight of the Garter. At court he displayed a pride and jealousy which led to quarrels with supposed rivals. At the time of the Armada the queen obliged him to remain in attendance on her at Tilbury, but in 1589 he flouted the queen's wishes and joined Drake and Norris in an expedition against Portugal. He distinguished himself by his recklessness in action but was speedily ordered home by the queen and soon restored to favour.

In 1590 he was once more in disfavour because of his clandestine marriage to Frances, daughter of the recently deceased Sir Francis Walsingham and widow of Sir Philip Sidney (plate 21). The queen was greatly angered by the marriage and not until Essex agreed virtually to banish his wife to the country was he forgiven. In July 1591 he received reluctant permission from the queen to command an expedition to France in support of Henri IV against the Catholic League. Again he became notorious for his recklessness and was finally recalled by the queen in January 1592 and, after the disgrace of Ralegh, became the queen's principal favourite.

The next four years were spent at court. In 1593 he was made a member of the Privy Council and began his association with Francis Bacon (plate 30) which was intended to be of political benefit to both. He failed, however, to obtain for Bacon either the office of Attorney-General or that of Solicitor-General, largely because of the opposition of Robert Cecil. Through Bacon's brother, Anthony, Essex maintained an extensive intelligence

BASIS VIRTVTV CONSTANTIA

EARLE MARSHAIL OF ENGLAND &c AND NOW LORDE GENERAIL OF HIR MA^{ties} FORCES IN IRLANDE

THE RIGHT HONO. THE E. OF ESSEX

William Rogers sculp.

VIRTVTIS COM—ES INVIDIA.

Are to be sould by Iohn

18 E.3317–1960

service in Europe and in 1594 was instrumental in exposing a Spanish plot to poison the queen.

In 1596 he secured the queen's agreement to command the land forces in a very powerful expedition which sailed from Plymouth at the beginning of June, his fellow commanders being Ralegh (plate 34), Lord Howard of Effingham (plate 15) and Lord Thomas Howard. The Spanish fleet was defeated off Cadiz on 20 June and Essex immediately landed and captured the town, an exploit which won general admiration. The expedition failed, however, to capture the Spanish treasure fleet but returned to Plymouth in August amidst general applause and with Essex a popular hero. It later appeared that had the fleet remained a few days longer as Essex had wished the capture of the treasure fleet could have been effected.

Attempting to follow Bacon's sound advice Essex appeared to wish to stay at home close to the queen and sought appointment to various offices, and in March 1597 was made Master of the Ordnance. Soon, against Bacon's advice, he was pressing for another command and in June 1597 was given a fleet of 20 ships and 6000 men for use against the Spanish treasure fleet and other shipping and for the seizure of the Azores. Because of this last aim the project is usually known as the Islands' Voyage. The initial attempt came to nothing because of severe storms, as was the case with a second attempt in August. In the event it was Ralegh, a subsidiary commander, who captured Fayal in the Azores, greatly to Essex's jealous indignation. The main treasure fleet was missed and it was only bad weather that dispersed a strong Spanish fleet and prevented an attack on the English expedition, which arrived home safely but with little booty.

The queen was displeased that so expensive an expedition had proved so unproductive and also by Essex's behaviour towards Ralegh. Essex was also jealous of Lord Howard of Effingham, the Lord Admiral, newly promoted to the earldom of Nottingham and given special praise for his services at Cadiz. In order to pacify Essex the queen appointed him Earl Marshal.

Cecil travelled on an embassy to France in 1598 and during his absence Essex was employed much more fully in the queen's official business, but this harmony was shattered by the queen's anger at the clandestine marriage of Essex's friend the Earl of Southampton (plate 19) in August 1598 and by reports of Essex's own improper relationships with no less than four ladies of the court.

From June 1598 there had been discussion in the council of the possibility of a peace with Spain. To this Essex was implacably opposed and the party for the continuance of the war eventually won the argument, to the displeasure of Lord Burghley and his son. In July the question of the appointment of a new Lord-Deputy in Ireland was under consideration. Essex rashly insulted the queen at a meeting of the council and was immediately struck on the ear by her, an episode which permanently soured their relationship. Burghley died on 4 August and Essex succeeded him as Chancellor of the University of Cambridge. His relatives and friends now urged him to make his peace with the queen and a reconciliation was achieved, with some reluctance on both sides, in October 1598. By this time revolt had broken out in Ireland and Essex foolishly allowed himself to be named for the post of commander in a campaign likely to prove difficult and possibly unsuccessful. The

queen was undecided for a time but in March 1599 appointed Essex commander and governor-general in Ireland. By mid-April he was in Dublin and in May he set out to subdue the province of Leinster. He was partially successful but exceeded his orders by venturing on into Munster. Returning to Dublin he found his army of 16,000 men reduced – by the provision of garrisons and by sickness and desertion – to little more than 4000. He had appointed his friend Southampton to be his general of horse but the queen would not approve the appointment. Essex was commanded to attack the rebels in Ulster and expressly forbidden to return to England without permission. The campaign did not go well and Essex was criticized by both the queen and the lords of the council. He had meetings with the rebel Earl of Tyrone early in September at which a truce was agreed. Elizabeth was incensed at this, writing angrily that no truce should be effected without prior consultation with her. At the end of September he rashly determined to appeal to the queen personally and hastened to London and then on to the Palace of Nonsuch in Surrey. The queen at first received him well but Cecil convinced her that action must be taken and charges preferred by the council, especially on the ground of his disobedience in leaving his post in Ireland. He was arrested and confined to York House where he became ill and although Cecil and the council were prepared to release him the queen remained unmoved, despite the considerable popular support for him. He was allowed to move to his own house to live there under the control of a gaoler. On 5 June he was brought before a specially constituted court at Essex House, consisting of all the senior officers of state and

the judges, and was charged with exceeding his orders, effecting a dishonourable treaty and abandoning his post. It seems he was also charged with the irregular appointment of Southampton and the over-lavish distribution of knighthoods. Francis Bacon was one of the prosecutors and behaved well towards his former patron. Essex was found guilty of contempt and disobedience and sentenced to be dismissed from all offices of state and to remain a prisoner in Essex House at the queen's pleasure. He was released, however, at the end of August.

The queen refused to see him or to reply to his submissive letters and he began to consider the possibility of removing by force those royal counsellors whom he considered to be his enemies. He discussed with Lords Southampton and Mountjoy (his successor as commander in Ireland) various near-treasonable possibilities and entered into negotiations with James VI of Scotland (plate 9) to establish James' right of succession to the throne of England with, of course, corresponding guarantees in respect of Essex's own position. Discussions went on between Essex and his discontented friends and followers, including several peers among whom Southampton was prominent. It was resolved that the Palace of Whitehall should be seized, that Essex should then see the queen and demand the dismissal of her existing council and the summoning of Parliament. However, before final details could be fixed, Essex heard early in February 1601 that the gist of his plot was known to the council and that he was to be summoned to appear before it. It was decided to take immediate action and the projected rising was fixed for Sunday 8 February 1601. Essex had been misled by Puritan zealots into believing that the city of London would rally to his support when called upon to do so. On 7 February 300 people assembled at Essex House, thus warning the council of immediate danger, so that early next morning the Lord Keeper, the Lord Chief Justice, the Earl of Worcester (plate 16) and Sir William Knollys, Essex's uncle, came to enquire into the reasons for such an assembly. They were immediately seized while Essex with 200 followers hurried into the city to rouse the people. The attempt failed entirely and Essex and his men withdrew, to be attacked and dispersed on Ludgate Hill by troops brought up by the Bishop of London. It was soon clear to Essex that he had no alternative but to surrender to the troops besieging Essex House. He was arrested and taken to the Tower, the queen issuing a proclamation thanking the citizenry for their loyalty.

On 19 February Essex was brought to trial in Westminster Hall before a special commission of 25 peers and nine judges. The case against him was overwhelming and Bacon, who spoke last for the prosecution, contributed largely to securing the final sentence of death. Essex denied that he had aimed to secure the throne for himself or had intended doing the queen any bodily injury. He confessed to his negotiations with Southampton and others and accused his secretary, Henry Cuffe, of encouraging him in his treasonable actions. He declined to beg for pardon and Lady Essex's attempts at intercession were unavailing. Cecil might have been prepared to recommend mercy but Ralegh wrote to him urging him not to relent. Elizabeth was deeply reluctant to sign the death warrant but eventually brought herself to do so on 24 February and Essex was beheaded on the following day.

He was buried in the chapel of St Peter-ad-Vincula in the Tower.

His execution was deeply regretted but accepted as inevitable in the circumstances. His popular reputation rested on his unswerving championship of England's interests against those of Spain, but his character was totally at variance with the responsibilities of one holding high office. He was vain, passionate, impulsive, reckless (although personally brave), politically immature and devoid of all judgment and discretion. Of extravagant habits he was invariably generous to his friends, many of whom were to be found in the world of literature and from whom he received many dedications. He was known as a writer of sonnets and of masques and as a lover of books. He is described by contemporaries as being tall, fair-complexioned and possessed of delicate hands.

Rogers' engraving seems to be based on Gheeraerts' portrait of c 1596, painted soon after Essex's return from the Cadiz expedition, which shows him wearing a beard. The portrait exists in numerous versions of which the best example is that at Woburn Abbey.

19 Henry Wriothesley, 3rd Earl of Southampton, KG (1573–1624)

Courtier and patron of literature

Engraving by Simon van de **Passe** published in 1617, probably freely based on a late portrait in oils.

(O'D 4; Hind: Part II, p.269, 54; R S, p.300)

19 E.3114–1960

Henry Wriothesley was the second son of Henry Wriothesley, 2nd Earl of Southampton, by his wife Mary Browne, daughter of the 1st Viscount Montague. He was born at Cowdray House, near Midhurst, Sussex, on 6 October 1573, and succeeded his father in 1581, his elder brother having predeceased him. Being aged only eight the new earl immediately became a royal ward and Elizabeth's minister Lord Burghley (plate 13) became his guardian.

At the age of 12 he was admitted to St John's College, Cambridge, where he remained for four years, receiving the degree of MA in 1589. He was entered as a student at Gray's Inn and became patron to John Florio, the Italian lexicographer and tutor, who taught him Italian. In 1590, when only 17, he was presented to the queen, received encouragement from her favourite Essex (plate 18) and enjoyed a great personal success at court with his many accomplishments and his physical beauty, which included striking auburn hair worn very long.

The earl's known love of literature caused many new works to be dedicated to him, including Florio's celebrated Italian-English dictionary which appeared in 1598. He is most celebrated, however, as the patron of William Shakespeare (plate 23) from whom he received the dedication of *Venus and Adonis* in 1593. Clearly a close relationship developed between Southampton and Shakespeare (who was nine-and-a-half years older than the earl), for the dedication of *The Rape of Lucrece*, which appeared in 1594, is expressed in terms of great personal friendship and devotion, as is also the case with the sentiments contained in many of Shakespeare's sonnets written about this time. It seems probable that Southampton behaved with great generosity to Shakespeare

and he did, in fact, remain Shakespeare's only acknowledged patron.

In 1595 the earl was involved in a liaison with Elizabeth Vernon, one of the queen's waiting-women, who was cousin to Essex. In consequence of adverse comment he withdrew from the court in 1596 and accompanied Essex on his expedition to the Azores, not returning until early in 1598. No sooner was he back than he became involved in a brawl in the queen's presence chamber and later in the year thought it advisable to accompany Sir Robert Cecil, the queen's secretary, on an embassy to Paris. Whilst in Paris he learned that Elizabeth Vernon was pregnant by him and briefly returned to England in order to marry her. The queen was greatly angered by this clandestine marriage and the circumstances which led up to it and had the new countess imprisoned, shortly to be followed by the earl on his return from the French embassy. The imprisonment of both did not last long, but Southampton by his scandalous behaviour had forfeited all hope of the queen's future favour.

He took himself to Ireland to join his friend Essex and the latter wished to give Southampton a major command there. The queen, however, refused to agree to it and Southampton returned to London where, avoiding the court, he sought diversion at the theatre which he is said to have attended every day. After Essex's arrest in 1599 Southampton became involved in a plot by which Essex hoped to restore his influence by rebellion. The plotters met frequently at Southampton's house and it was he who was responsible for procuring the players at the Globe Theatre to perform, as a provocation, Shakespeare's *Richard II* (its subject being the deposition of a king) on the evening preceding the unsuccessful attempt at

rebellion on 8 February 1601. Southampton was tried for treason along with Essex and was duly sentenced to death. By Cecil's intervention, however, the sentence was commuted to life imprisonment.

On the accession of James I Southampton was immediately released from the Tower. He returned to court and received many new honours. His forfeited earldom was recreated, he was made Captain of the Isle of Wight and Lord-Lieutenant of Hampshire, given the Order of the Garter and received various minor posts. He was favoured by the new queen but again his impetuous and reckless character soon led him into trouble, for he quarrelled publicly with Lord Gray in the queen's presence and was sent once more briefly to the Tower. The king and queen continued to look on him with favour, however, but Cecil – now Lord Salisbury and the king's first minister – distrusted him and saw to it that he was given no office of real influence. Southampton turned his mind and his very considerable wealth to colonial undertakings. He became a member of both the Virginia and the East India companies and was closely concerned with the North-West Passage company.

Although brought up as a Catholic Southampton later adopted the Protestant cause, most notably in the defence of the Elector Palatine and his wife, the former English Princess Elizabeth (plate 12), against the attacks of their Catholic enemies. In 1614 the earl fought as a volunteer for the Protestant cause in Cleves in North Germany.

In 1617 Southampton attended the king on a long visit to Scotland which appeared to confirm him in royal favour, for in 1619 he became a member of the Privy Council. As a member of the council he was seen to be at the centre of the opposition to the king's favourite, Buckingham. He was eager to provide effective assistance to the Elector Palatine (now also King of Bohemia) who was defeated by the Imperial forces at the Battle of Prague in 1620, believing, with justification, that both the king and Buckingham were neglectful of the Elector's interests. His opposition was such that he was arrested in June 1621 and detained for a month before being ordered to retire to his Hampshire estate at Titchfield.

In the 1624 session of Parliament Southampton was again very active, devoting himself particularly to the defence of the Virginia company in the face of Spanish complaints. His efforts were, however, in vain for the company's charter was withdrawn in June 1624. In the summer he and his elder son went to the Low Countries in command of a troop of English volunteers against the forces of the emperor. There they both fell victims to fever and Southampton's son was the first to die. He himself eventually died at Bergen-op-Zoom on 10 November 1624. The bodies were brought back to England and buried at Titchfield at the end of December.

Southampton was one of the most frequently portrayed men of his generation. This engraved portrait shows him at the height of his powers in 1617.

20   E.1577–1960

20   Sir Henry Brooke Cobham (1538–1605?)

Diplomatist

Engraving, dated 1582, probably by Remigius **Hogenberg.**

(Not in O'D or Hind)

Sir Henry Brooke Cobham was the fifth son of George Brooke, 6th Baron Cobham, and his wife Anne, daughter of John, 2nd Baron Braye. He assumed the surname of Cobham from his father's title and was known by that name throughout his career.

As early as 1561 he accompanied the English ambassador to Madrid, returning to England with despatches later in the year. In 1567 he was sent as an envoy to Vienna on a mission to determine the possibility or otherwise of re-opening marriage negotiations between Queen Elizabeth and the Archduke Charles. In 1570 he was despatched on a complicated mission to Antwerp, Speyer (where he was received by the Emperor), Paris and, finally, Spain where he was grudgingly received by Philip II as an envoy extraordinary. He attempted to negotiate on the seizure of English ships by Spain, in retaliation for English attacks on and seizure of Spanish shipping, and for the expulsion from Spain of English Catholics who had sought refuge there. In the end, however, he was obliged to return to England without achieving anything.

He was knighted in the summer of 1575 and, later in that year, was again sent to Madrid to seek – with the threat of war – religious toleration for English subjects resident in or travelling through Spain and for English ambassadors to be allowed to use Anglican forms of worship in their own houses. He also offered mediation between Philip II and his rebellious subjects in the Netherlands. Cobham's mission met with little success; the offer of mediation was refused and only some slight relaxation of the anti-heresy laws in favour of English residents was reluctantly conceded. On his return to England he was immediately sent to Brussels to threaten war if further coercive measures against the Protestants were undertaken.

In 1579 he succeeded Sir Amyas Paulet as ambassador in Paris with instructions to negotiate for a joint expedition to place Don Antonio on the throne of Portugal, for the relief of English subjects whose commercial interests were damaged by French privateers and to play for time over the matter of·the queen's proposed marriage to the Duke of Alençon. In 1581 he was joined by two other ambassadors (one of whom was Francis Walsingham) to urge on the French king the conclusion of a treaty of friendship between France and England in place of the Alençon marriage.

In 1583 he was recalled from Paris and subsequently sat as MP for Kent in the Parliaments of 1586 and 1589. He was still living in 1604 but it seems likely that his death occurred soon afterwards.

He was married to Anne, daughter of Sir Henry Sutton, by whom he had three sons. From the date of the engraving (1582) it would appear that this portrait was published during the period of Cobham's embassy to Paris. In style it is close to Remigius Hogenberg's portrait of Archbishop Parker which is dated 1572.

21 Sir Philip Sidney (1554–1586)

Soldier, statesman and poet

Engraving by Renold **Elstrack,** probably after a portrait by John De **Critz.**

(O'D 18; Hind: Part II, pp.189–190, 55; R S; p.292)

Philip Sidney was born at Penshurst Place, Sussex, on 30 November 1554, the eldest son of Sir Henry Sidney, Lord Deputy of Ireland, and his wife Mary Dudley, daughter of the

21   E.1702–1888

1st Duke of Northumberland and sister to Robert Dudley, Earl of Leicester (plate 14). He was educated at Shrewsbury School and Christ Church, Oxford, showing himself, despite his somewhat delicate health, to be a lover of learning from the earliest age. Through his father he was acquainted as a boy with the great Secretary of State, Sir William Cecil (plate 13), who became very fond of him. In 1569–70 a marriage was arranged between Sidney and Cecil's daughter Anne but the negotiations were eventually abandoned. Early in 1571, with the outbreak of the plague in Oxford, Sidney left the university without taking his degree.

He paid frequent visits to court and in May 1572 received permission from the queen to spend two years abroad to improve his knowledge of languages. He spent some months in Paris at the French court where he was well received, but after the Massacre of St Bartholomew on 23 August 1572 Lord Burghley and his uncle Leicester both instructed the English ambassador in Paris to obtain passports for Sidney so that he might leave the country. He travelled to Frankfurt where in 1572 he met the great scholar Hubert Languet who became a profound influence on his life. With Languet he visited Vienna and the court of the Emperor Maximilian II, also travelling on into Hungary. He later went to Italy, spending much of his time in Venice where he came to know, among many others, the painters Tintoretto and Veronese, the latter of whom painted his portrait. Having fallen seriously ill in Venice he returned – after his recovery – to Languet in Vienna and subsequently accompanied him on a journey into Poland. Throughout this time his attachment to the Protestant cause became stronger and stronger. In December 1574 he sent to Burghley from Vienna a survey of the political situation in eastern Europe and apparently undertook some diplomatic duties. In February 1575 he accompanied the Emperor's train to Prague and while there was summoned home to England, malicious rumour having declared that he had turned Catholic. He obeyed the summons but took the opportunity to visit various scholars on his way, arriving in London in June 1575.

Leicester did his best to advance Sidney's interests at court. He became acquainted with the 1st Earl of Essex and accompanied him to Ireland to visit his father Sir Henry Sidney. Lord Essex died in Ireland, expressing a death-bed wish that Philip Sidney should marry his daughter Penelope. Sidney began to write his long series of sonnets addressed to the Lady Penelope under the courtly name of Stella. At first his attraction to her seems to have had a conventionally courtly character but as time passed affection developed and after Penelope's marriage to Lord Rich in 1581 his feelings seem to have taken on a strongly passionate character.

Early in 1577 Sidney was sent by the queen on a diplomatic mission to the Elector Palatine and to the new Emperor Rudolph II, with the avowed principal intentions of attempting the reconciliation of the Lutherans and the Calvinists in the Palatinate, of recovering various loans made by Elizabeth to the late Elector and congratulating the Emperor on his accession. He also did all that he could to stimulate interest in the formation of a league of Protestant princes. He returned to England early in June and actively defended to the queen his father's activities in Ireland, currently under severe criticism from his enemies.

Sidney's influence at court continued to grow but his circle of friends extended well beyond the limits of the court to embrace a wide variety of literary men, artists, musicians and skilled craftsmen. It was at this time that his friendship developed with the poet Edmund Spenser, marked in 1579 by the latter's dedication of his 'The Shepherd's Calendar' to Sidney. He also concerned himself with the activities of his uncle Leicester's company of actors and with the defence of the theatre against Puritan attack.

He found constant attendance at court tedious and spent part of 1579 superintending the extensions to his father's house at Penshurst. He experienced, in any case, a share of the queen's disfavour because of Leicester's marriage in 1578 (revealed to the queen in August 1579), his own quarrel with the Earl of Oxford and his submission of a memorandum arguing strongly against the queen's proposed marriage to the Duke of Anjou. During the period of his exclusion from court he visited his sister, the Countess of Pembroke, at Wilton where he wrote his celebrated 'Arcadia' for her amusement. At the end of October 1580 he was eventually allowed to return to court and in January 1581 was elected MP for the county of Kent.

On 13 January 1583 he was knighted to enable him adequately to fulfil his role as proxy for Prince John Casimir of the Palatinate at the latter's institution as a Knight of the Garter. Shortly afterwards, in order to provide him with an income, he became effectively joint Master of the Ordnance, serving with his uncle Lord Warwick, a post confirmed in 1585 when he was also appointed a 'general of horse'. In September 1583 he married Frances Walsingham, daughter of the

Secretary of State, Sir Francis Walsingham. The couple seem to have shared a mutual affection, but Sidney's life-long devotion to Penelope Rich continued to find expression in his verse.

About this time he turned his attention to the possibility of becoming involved in the colonization of North America, interesting himself in various schemes in turn. In the autumn of 1584 Sidney was sent as ambassador to France to convey the queen's condolences to Henri III on the death of his brother the Duke of Anjou, and to attempt to discover whether the king was prepared to oppose the advance of the Spaniards in the Low Countries. The embassy was unsuccessful, but Sidney sent much sound advice to the queen, recommending that immediate attacks be made on Spanish ports and on Spain's American trade. The queen, however, decided to send an army into the Low Countries to support the Protestants. Sidney attempted to join Drake's expedition against Spain but was prevented from doing so by the queen.

In November 1585 he was appointed Governor of Flushing when Leicester became commander-in-chief in the Netherlands. On arriving at Flushing Sidney found the garrison dispirited and short of supplies. He also found it impossible to bring either Leicester or the queen to appreciate the necessity for swift and resolute action in the field and the situation was further vitiated by squabbles over commands.

Sidney's father and mother died in May and August of 1586 respectively. In July he organized a daring raid which captured the village of Axel and on 22 September he took a gallant – if foolhardy – part in the Battle of Zutphen. He was wounded in the left leg and removed to Arnhem where his wife came to nurse him. The wound refused to heal, however, and he eventually died from it on 17 October. The body was brought to London for burial but difficulties over his debts delayed the ceremony and it was not until 16 February 1587, amidst universal mourning, that a ceremonial military internment took place in St Paul's Cathedral. The event was recorded in a series of 34 engravings by Thomas Lant. His widow lived until 1632, having married in 1590 Robert Devereux, 2nd Earl of Essex (plate 18), and subsequently the 4th Earl of Clanricarde.

None of Sidney's writings was published in his lifetime, although most were known to a limited public through the circulation of manuscript copies. The highly-mannered 'Arcadia' (first published in 1590) is deeply indebted to Italian and Spanish romances, and to other foreign literary sources. It proved immensely popular with 16th- and 17th-century readers, having a great influence on contemporary literature. Sidney's collection of 108 sonnets and 11 songs, dating from c 1575 to c 1583, entitled 'Astrophel and Stella', was first published in an incomplete edition in 1591. Sidney's critical essay 'An Apologie for Poetrie' (later called 'The Defence of Poesie') was written in 1579, largely in refutation of an attack on the stage and in defence of imaginative literature, and was first published in 1595. The verse translations of the psalms undertaken by Sidney and his sister Lady Pembroke were not published until the 19th century.

Sidney was regarded by his contemporaries as an outstanding English patriot, a Protestant hero and a man of great talents in many fields. Clearly his personality was extremely engag-ing and won admiration from all who met him, although evidence on his personal appearance is somewhat contradictory, coming as it does from commentators who did not know him in life. Ben Jonson remarked that he was 'no pleasant man in countenance, his face having been spoiled with pimples & of high blood & long'; this disfiguration had been caused by smallpox when he was six. John Aubrey, however, recorded that 'He was not only of an excellent wit, but extremely beautiful; he much resembled his sister, but his hair was not red, but a little inclining, viz. a dark amber colour'.

The engraving by Elstrack is probably after a portrait by John de Critz of which several versions exist.

22 George Chapman (1559?–1634)

Poet, dramatist and translator of Homer

Engraving by William **Hole**. Frontispiece to Chapman's *The Whole Works of Homer Prince of Poetts in his Illiads and Odysses . . .* , published by N Butter, London, 1616.

(O'D 1; Hind: Part II, p.318, 3)

The circumstances of George Chapman's early life are obscure. He was probably born near Hitchin, Hertfordshire, in about 1559, and the antiquarian Anthony Wood claims that he was educated at Oxford but left without taking a degree.

His first publication appeared in 1594 with two verse *Hymns*. These were followed in 1595 by four other poems of varying merit, including *Ovid's Banquet of Sense*, and 1596 saw the publication of a lengthy prefatory poem to Laurence Kemys' *A Relation of the Second Voyage to Guiana* (that undertaken for Walter Ralegh), which associates Chapman clearly with the celebration of contemporary English valour and achievements. In 1598 he published a completion of Marlowe's *Hero and Leander* in which he acknowledged the patronage of Lady Walsingham.

By 1596 he was also a successful writer for the stage and the 'Diary' of the theatrical manager Philip Henslowe records in February of that year the first production of Chapman's *The Blind Beggar of Alexandria*. His name appears repeatedly in Henslowe's accounts until 1599 when it is suggested that he temporarily abandoned the theatre in order to concentrate upon his translation of Homer. It is also thought likely, however, that he was at that time engaged upon writing masques for performance by the Children of the Chapel. In 1599 his most celebrated comedy *All Fools* was played, although it was not published until 1605.

Chapman published the first instalment of his translation of the *Iliad* in 1598 and in his dedication to the Earl of Essex (plate 18) he referred to his current financial difficulties. Later in that year appeared the translation of Book 18, entitled *Achilles Shield*. There was subsequently a long wait for the publication of the completed translation of the first 12 books of the poem, which finally appeared some 10 years later in an undated edition, probably of 1609, bearing a dedication to his new patron the young Prince Henry (plate 11). It seems likely that the prince's encouragement speeded the work for the complete ver-

22   E.1584(2)–1960

sion of the *Iliad* was registered at Stationers' Hall on 8 April 1611.

Chapman seems to have embarked at once on the translation of the *Odyssey* and the work went ahead rapidly, despite the death of Prince Henry in November 1612. The first 12 books appeared together, and the completed translation of the 24 books was registered by the London publisher Nathaniel Butter on 2 November 1614. The work was dedicated to Chapman's new patron, Robert Carr, Earl of Somerset. The translations of the two great poems were issued together by Butter in a folio volume in 1616 and it is from that edition that the engraved portrait comes. Finally, in about 1624, Chapman brought his Homeric translations to a conclusion by publishing a version of the *Batrachomyomachia*.

Although the translations have been criticized for their errors they undoubtedly represent Chapman's greatest contribution to the culture of the times, having a vigour and freshness which undoubtedly stirred many imaginations before that of the poet Keats. Chapman's achievement was apparent to his contemporaries and he received recognition and praise – but apparently little profit – during his lifetime.

Chapman resumed his career as a playwright in 1605 with *Eastward Hoe*, a play written in collaboration with Ben Jonson and John Marston, which caused the authors to be imprisoned and threatened with other punishments for the satires against the Scots which it contained. In 1606 appeared both *The Gentleman Usher* and *Monsieur d'Olive*, to be followed in 1607 by his well-known tragedy of *Bussy d'Ambois*, which achieved great popularity in its day. It is one of a series of plays written about personages and events in recent French history which appeared between 1605 and about 1613 and which seems to have been very well received. His comedies *May Day* and *The Widow's Tears* appeared in 1611 and 1612 respectively, but after that date Chapman seems to have produced little. A play called *The Ball*, written in collaboration with James Shirley, was licensed as late as 1632 and the tragedy of *Caesar and Pompey* was published in 1631, although recorded as having been written many years earlier.

Chapman seems to have been industrious and esteemed by his contemporaries, but to have had little material success in his career. He may, perhaps, have been unfortunate in his patrons, in that Prince Henry died young and that the Earl of Somerset was disgraced in 1615. Whatever the reasons he seems to have been constantly in need of money and there are many references to his poverty throughout his writings. He died in London on 12 May 1634 and was buried in the churchyard of St Giles-in-the-Fields where a monument designed by his friend Inigo Jones was erected to his memory.

Anthony Wood described Chapman as being 'a person of most reverent aspect, religious and temperate, qualities rarely meeting in a poet'. The portrait by Hole, depicting the poet in his mid-50s, seems to illustrate this judgment well.

23 E.617–1960

23 William Shakespeare (1564–1616)

Dramatist and poet

Engraving by Martin **Droeshout.** Used on the title-page of the First Folio edition of 1623.

(O'D 4; Hind: Part II, p.354, 11, 4th state; R S, p.283)

The dramatist was born on 23 April 1564 at Stratford-on-Avon, Warwickshire, the first son and third child of John Shakespeare, a prosperous dealer in all types of agricultural products who was sometimes described as a butcher and sometimes as a glover and clearly had interests in more than one trade. Shakespeare's mother was Mary Arden, a member of an old and prosperous Warwickshire family. John Shakespeare's own prosperity appears to have continued until at least 1575 when he was still buying property in Stratford, having been chief alderman of the town in 1571–72, but by 1578 he was experiencing financial difficulties and in 1586 was deprived of his office of alderman. Shakespeare was a pupil at the town's free grammar school, probably from 1571 to about 1577, and from that date until his marriage he may well have worked for his father. Late in 1582 he married Anne, daughter of Richard Hathaway, a prosperous yeoman, she being his senior by eight years. In May 1583 their eldest child, Susanna, was born. Twins, Hamnet and Judith, were born early in 1585 and it seems probable that later in that year Shakespeare left Stratford, possibly in consequence of some poaching activities, and lived mainly apart from his wife and family for the next 11 years.

He apparently soon found employment in and around the London theatres and eventually made a reputation as an actor, probably with the Earl of Leicester's company which in time became the Lord Chamberlain's company. Among the leading players who became his friends were Richard Burbage, John Heming and Henry Condell. The company played originally at the Theatre in Shoreditch, appearing subsequently at the Rose on Bankside, the Curtain in Shoreditch and, from 1599, at the Globe on Bankside. The London companies of actors travelled into the provinces and even into Europe, paying visits to foreign courts as opportunities arose, although there is no evidence of Shakespeare travelling abroad.

His first essays as a dramatist probably date from 1591 and his output extended over the next 20 years. During that period he produced almost 40 plays, most of them of major significance. His first original play, as opposed to those by others which may have been subjected to his revision, was almost certainly *Love's Labours Lost* of 1591. This was first published in 1598 bearing, for the first time, Shakespeare's name as an author on its title-page. Plays followed one another in rapid succession, *Richard III* and *Richard II* both reflecting the influence of Christopher Marlowe who was killed in 1593. Shakespeare's poem *Venus and Adonis* was published in London in 1593 by his friend from Stratford, Richard Field, and in the following year appeared his poem *The Rape of Lucrece*, also printed by Field and published by John Harrison. Both poems were dedicated to the Earl of Southampton (plate 19). They proved to be very popular and undoubtedly did much to establish Shakespeare's reputation with the public. He appears to have become something of a favourite with the queen and to have acted before her frequently. The *Sonnets* were probably composed between 1591 and 1597, although they were not published until 1609, and are closely related to Shakespeare's friendship with Lord Southampton. *A Midsummer Night's Dream* was probably written in 1594 and played either late in that year or very early in 1595. It was followed by *Henry IV: Parts I and II*, *The Merry Wives of Windsor* and *Henry V* in 1598 – virtually the last of the histories.

Shakespeare's reputation stood high in the London theatre and contemporary comment by Francis Meres and Richard Barnfield in 1598 was of the most flattering kind and it is clear that by this date his fortunes were on a sound footing. His father's business difficulties had continued since his son's departure from Stratford and it seems likely that he retired from trade in 1595. Probably in the following year Shakespeare returned to Stratford to re-establish the family fortunes. Actions against his father for the recovery of debts cease from that year and Shakespeare seems to have lived in Stratford with his wife and family for at least part of each subsequent year. In August 1596 his only son Hamnet died and was buried in the parish church. Later in the year his father, doubtless at Shakespeare's instigation, applied to the College of Arms for a grant of arms. The application was not pursued, however, and it was not until three years later that the matter was re-opened. In May 1597 Shakespeare took a major step to re-assert his family's pretensions by buying the largest house in the town, New Place. Repair work was carried out on the house almost at once but he does not seem to have settled there per-

manently until 1611. His father died in 1601 and Shakespeare continued to extend his interests by the purchase of additional land and a part interest in the tithes of the town until he clearly ranked as Stratford's leading citizen.

The years of ever-increasing prosperity and social stability between 1597 and 1603 saw the production of some of his finest work in both tragedy and comedy, including *Julius Caesar*, *Hamlet*, *Twelfth Night* and *As You Like It*. His company, the Lord Chamberlain's Men, remained popular with Queen Elizabeth until her death and on the accession of James I the position was even improved by the grant of a new licence and the new designation of the company as The King's Servants. Shakespeare's plays were frequently performed at court as well as at the Globe Theatre and it seems probable that the increase in patronage led to a corresponding impetus in his creativity. The new reign saw the early production of both *Othello* and *Measure for Measure* in 1604. The two following years produced *Macbeth*, written in deference to the king's Scottish ancestry, and *King Lear*, which was played before the court at Whitehall on 26 December 1606. A sequence of major works brought Shakespeare's dramatic output to its close, apparently in 1611. *Antony and Cleopatra* and *Coriolanus* both seem to date from 1608, while *Cymbeline* of 1610–11, *A Winter's Tale* of 1611 and *The Tempest*, probably also of 1611, bring his career as a dramatist to a stately conclusion in an aura of calm reconciliation.

The remaining years of Shakespeare's life appear to have been mainly spent at Stratford. His plays continued to be performed at court, in fact during the festivities at the wedding of the Princess Elizabeth (plate 12) and the

Elector Palatine in May 1613 no less than seven of them were presented. He featured prominently in various local matters in Stratford during these last years but early in 1616 he began to experience the ill-health which eventually culminated in his death, caused by a fever, on 23 April 1616 – his 52nd birthday. He was buried in Stratford Parish Church on 24 April, being survived by his wife (who lived until 1623) and his two married daughters and heiresses, Susanna Hall and Judith Quiney.

Aubrey says that Shakespeare was 'a handsome, well-shap't man', while Ben Jonson in professing his affection for him declares that 'He was, indeed, honest and of an open and free nature'.

Sixteen of the plays were published separately during his lifetime, usually in unauthorized editions with incomplete or corrupt texts. The first collected edition was the First Folio edition of 1623, containing 36 pieces, which was prepared by his former actor colleagues John Heming and Henry Condell. The engraved portrait by Martin Droeshout was used on the title-page of the First Folio and, subsequently, in the Second and Third Folio editions of 1632 and 1663 respectively. The present example is taken from the Fourth Folio of 1685.

ANNO DNI. 1591.

*This was for youth, Strength, Mirth, and wit that Time :
Most count their golden Age; but t'was not thine.
Thine was thy later yeares, so much refind
From youths Drosse, Mirth, & witt; as thy pure mind
Thought (like the Angels) nothing but the Praise
Of thy Creator, in those last, best Dayes.
Witnes this Booke, (thy Embleme) which begins
With Love; but endes, with Sighes, & Teares for sins.*

Will: Marshall: sculpsit.

24   E.2387-1960

24   **John Donne (1572–1631)**

Poet and divine; Dean of St Paul's Cathedral

Engraving by William **Marshall** after a lost miniature portrait of 1591 by Nicholas **Hilliard**. Frontispiece to the editions of his *Poems* published in 1635 and 1639.

(O'D 8; C and N 30; R S, p.66 and plate 119)

John Donne in his youth and middle years was the most subtle of poets and in his later years the most captivating of preachers. His extraordinary imaginative achievements in both these roles were the products not only of his genius and learning but also of the powerful religious, intellectual and political pressures which were with him throughout his life.

Born the son of a wealthy Catholic tradesman in London he inherited a family tradition of Catholicism, literature and the law. His mother's grandmother was a sister of Sir Thomas More, her father was the dramatist John Heywood and two of his uncles were Jesuit priests. Throughout his youth and early manhood Donne was subject to the tensions inherent in the sour politico-religious situation and in the unresolved conflict between medieval and modern patterns of thought. In 1570 had occurred the excommunication of Queen Elizabeth with all that this implied for increased antagonism between the ascendant Protestantism and the old Catholicism of England.

He studied at both Oxford and Cambridge but, being a Catholic, he was unable to take a degree, proceeding instead to study law at Lincoln's Inn.

He subsequently sailed with the Earl of Essex (plate 18) on the Cadiz expedition of 1596 and in 1597 became secretary to Lord Keeper Egerton. However, a clandestine marriage with Egerton's niece ruined his career and for 14 years he and his wife lived in poverty. His study of theology in this period led him eventually to a position where he found himself opposed to the extremes of both Calvin and Rome and in 1615, largely as a result of King James' interest in his theological writings in defence of the reformed position, Donne was ordained into the Anglican priesthood. He found swift advancement in the Church, becoming immediately a chaplain to the king, Divinity Reader at Lincoln's Inn in 1616 and Dean of St Paul's in 1621. He was a celebrated and moving preacher and a conscientious administrator, remaining in his deanery until his death on 31 March 1631. He was buried in the cathedral and his remarkable effigy by Nicholas Stone, which depicts him in his shroud, was the only major sculpture to escape destruction in the Great Fire. It may now be seen in the South Choir Aisle, appropriately placed next to the doorway of the Dean's vestry.

Little of his poetry, certainly none of his early love poems and satires, was printed in his lifetime, although much became well known from the manuscript copies which circulated widely among his admirers. In 1612 he wrote a funeral elegy on Prince Henry (plate 11) and in 1613 he published an *Epithalamium* on the marriage of Princess Elizabeth (plate 12) to the Count Palatine. The first full edition of his *Poems* was published in 1633 with an *Elegie* by his friend Isaac Walton. This penetrating portrait by Nicholas Hilliard, showing him as a youth of 18, was engraved to serve as frontispiece to the succeeding editions of 1635 and 1639, the verses below the portrait being by Isaac Walton.

25 E.3316–1960

Herbalist and surgeon

Engraving by William **Rogers**. Frontispiece to the first edition of the *Herball* in 1597.

(Not in O'D; Hind: Part I, p.268, no. 11, 2nd state; R S, p.127 and plate 252)

John Gerard was born in 1545 at Nantwich in Cheshire and was educated locally, subsequently studying medicine, and in later years travelling to Scandinavia, Russia and, possibly, to the Mediterranean area.

In 1562 he was apprenticed to a leading London surgeon and in 1569 was admitted to the freedom of the Barber-Surgeons' Company. His career clearly prospered for by 1595 he had become a senior member of the company and was superintendent of Lord Burghley's gardens, both at his town house in the Strand and at his estate of Theobalds in Hertfordshire, a property which was later to belong to James I who died there. In the following year he published a catalogue of the plants then to be found in his own garden in Holborn, this being the first published catalogue of any garden. In August 1597 he became Junior Warden of the Barber-Surgeons' Company and attempted to establish through the company a garden in London for the study of medicinal herbs, a plan which unfortunately came to nothing.

In December 1597 his celebrated work *The Herball, or a Generall Historie of Plantes* was published in London by John Norton. The book, dedicated to his patron Lord Burghley (plate 13) established his fame. Although adapted from Rembert Dodoens' *Stirpium historiae pemptades* of 1583 and illustrated with woodcuts originally used in a book published in Frankfurt in 1590 the *Herball* contains much original material concerning British plants and related matters. It had great influence and was reprinted twice in the 17th century, in 1633 and 1636. In legal documents of 1605 Gerard is described as 'herbarist' to the king and in 1607 he received the ultimate honour from the Barber-Surgeons when he was elected master of the company. He died in February 1612 and was buried in St Andrew's Church, Holborn.

This engraving by Rogers is the only authentic portrait known.

26 **William Butler** (**1535–1618**)

Physician

Engraving by Simon van de **Passe**, published in 1620.

(O'D 1; Hind: Part II, p.253, no. 14)

William Butler was born in Ipswich and received his university education at Cambridge. The records are not entirely clear but it seems that he might be the William Butler who entered Peterhouse in 1558, became BA and a fellow of the college in 1561 and proceeded to MA in 1564. He subsequently became a fellow of Clare Hall (later Clare College) and was licensed by the university to practise as a physician in 1572, although he never in fact took the degree of doctor of medicine. He acquired, nevertheless, a great

26 E.3107–1960

reputation in his profession both for his prescribing and for his unorthodox treatments, some of which are amusingly recalled by John Aubrey.

In 1612 he was called from Cambridge to attend Henry, Prince of Wales (plate 11) during his last illness. Two years later he treated the king for the effects of a fall received when he was out hunting at Newmarket. The king was so grateful to the aged physician that he honoured him with a private visit when he came to Cambridge in May 1615.

Butler seems to have led a somewhat eccentric bachelor existence and when he died on 29 January 1618 he left the bulk of his estate – apart from a generous bequest to Clare – to his old friend the Cambridge apothecary John Crane. He is buried in the University Church of Great St Mary's where a contemporary monument describes him as the most distinguished physician of his time.

27 **Sir Thomas Gresham** (**1519?–1579**)

Merchant, financier, diplomat and founder of the Royal Exchange

Engraving by Francis **Delaram** after a portrait possibly by Adrian **Key**.

(O'D 11; Hind: Part II, p.223, 14, 1st state; R S, p.130)

Thomas Gresham, the second son of Sir Richard Gresham, Lord Mayor of London in 1537–38, and his wife Audrey Lynn, was born in London probably early in 1519. He was

EQVI. AVRA. VIVA EFFIGIES PRECLAR^M DOM THOMÆ GRESHAM

Francies Delarasti Sculp

The lively portraiture of y^e most worthy Citizen, Sr Thomas
Gresham, who amongst many of his acte (whereby he hath eter=
nized his never dying fame) did at his owne propper costes y^t
Royal Exchange of London Also He founded a colledg, and
endowed it with livings for 7 learned men, for y^e
reading of y^e 7 liberall sciences. &c.   Ar^e to be sould by
Io: Sudbu: & G Humb

27   E.356–1960

educated at Gonville and Caius College, Cambridge, and after leaving the university was apprenticed to his uncle, the London merchant Sir John Gresham, and also became a student of Gray's Inn. In 1543 he was admitted to the freedom of the Mercers' Company, to which both his father and his uncle belonged, and was apparently in that same year already acting as an agent for the king in the Low Countries. He married Anne Read (born Ferneley), widow of a fellow mercer, in 1544 and at his father's death in 1549 established himself at the famous sign of the grasshopper (his family's crest) in Lombard Street in the city of London.

His business took him abroad a great deal and in 1551 he was given the important appointment of Royal Agent or King's Merchant at Antwerp. The principal responsibilities of this office were to negotiate foreign loans on behalf of the crown, to make purchases for the state (especially of armaments) and to keep the Privy Council in London informed on all matters of international importance. Gresham was obliged to travel to London frequently and in order to maintain a good intelligence service he employed agents throughout Europe. As a result of his operations Gresham, within a very few years, had greatly increased the exchange rate for the English pound and because of this had begun the task of discharging the king's enormous foreign debts.

Gresham was on very good terms with the young King Edward and in 1552 was employed on some very delicate diplomatic affairs with the Emperor and with the Regent of the Netherlands. Just before the king's death in 1553 Gresham received from him very substantial grants of land, especially in Norfolk. With the accession of Mary I (plate 1) his fortunes suffered a reverse and as a known Protestant he was briefly removed from his office of Royal Agent. His successor proved to be so disastrously incompetent, however, that the Council eventually asked him to resume the office, virtually on his own terms. He renewed his activities with great success. These included the smuggling of gold from the Netherlands at the behest of the Privy Council and a journey to Spain in 1554 to obtain a loan of 500,000 ducats in gold.

Queen Mary died on 17 November 1558 and Sir William Cecil (plate 13), an old friend of Gresham, became the new queen's secretary-of-state. Elizabeth received Gresham with favour, continuing him in office. Soon he was advising the queen on methods of improving her finances, of which the most important recommendations were to borrow as little as possible from abroad and to restore the purity of the coinage – this latter advice later to be formulated as 'Gresham's Law' in the economic maxim that 'bad money drives out good'. His financial advice was always well received by Cecil and the Council and for the next nine years he continued to divide his time between London and Antwerp, his influence being considerable in both cities.

In 1559 he was appointed ambassador to the Duchess of Parma, the Spanish Regent of the Netherlands, and was knighted before he set out early in 1560. He maintained a secret correspondence with Cecil and was responsible for the transmission of much important political information while at the same time pursuing his business of raising loans and procuring arms. He also became actively involved in the vital business of reforming the currency and in 1561–62 was concerning himself with the more efficient management of the London customs service. His final visit to Antwerp was made in March 1567 and coincided with the first battle between the Protestants and the forces of the Regent. Gresham finally left for home on 19 April and from henceforth he was to live permanently in England. He had splendid houses at Mayfield in Sussex and Osterley in Middlesex as well as three other houses in Norfolk and Suffolk. His London home was at Gresham House in Bishopsgate Street where he maintained a lavish style of living.

Gresham continued to be actively involved in affairs of state, attempting to find adequate financial solutions to various problems. In 1569 he advised the Council to raise in London the necessary loans which had previously been raised abroad. Through his insistence and energetic advice this was achieved, although he continued to complain at the government's unpunctuality in repayment which so damaged the queen's credit with the London merchants. Increasing infirmity caused him to turn more and more of his foreign business to the care of agents and in May 1574 he ceased to be the Queen's Agent, selling his house in Antwerp later in the year.

His only son, Richard, died in 1564 and it seems that Gresham then turned his thoughts towards using some of his great wealth to benefit the city of London. Gresham's father had cherished in the 1530s a scheme for the erection of an exchange for use by the city merchants but the project had come to nothing. In January 1565 Gresham offered to build such an exchange at his own expense if the city would provide a site. This was found at the junction of Cornhill and Threadneedle Street and Gresham laid the foundation stone on 7 June 1566. The building was designed by a Flemish architect and many of the building materials were imported from Antwerp. It closely resembled the exchange in that city and was ready for use in December 1568. In January 1571 the queen paid an official visit to the building and named it the Royal Exchange.

Another enterprise which Gresham put in hand at the close of 1574 or early in 1575 was the establishment of a college in the city with free lectures open to all who chose to attend. Despite opposition from the University of Cambridge Gresham persisted with his plan, bequeathing for this purpose his house in Bishopsgate Street and the rents which he received from the shops in the Royal Exchange. The bequests were to be vested jointly in the Corporation of London and the Mercers' Company who were to appoint seven lecturers who were to provide the necessary instruction. In addition to these benefactions Gresham also established almshouses in the city close to his own residence. His death came suddenly from a stroke on 21 November 1579 and he was buried with great splendour in the Church of Great St Helen's, Bishopsgate.

Gresham was a man of great shrewdness and energy and a loyal servant to Queen Elizabeth. His services were incalculable in improving the queen's credit abroad, in improving the purity of the English currency and in freeing the queen from a vast burden of foreign debt. Although it has been shown that he was not above some sharp practice in mingling his own commercial affairs with those of the state he, nevertheless, clearly had a high reputation for honest dealing and high commercial ability with both the merchants of Antwerp and the queen's Privy Council, as is evidenced by the great and continuing trust which was put in him.

In appearance Gresham was above middle height and of grave and courteous manners. It is clear that he was also of cultivated tastes in architecture, literature and music. The engraving is based on an oil portrait of c 1565, possibly by Adrian Key.

SVTTONVM ingenium et locupletem industria fecit
Congestas miseris ille refudit opes

28 E.3144–1960

28 Thomas Sutton
(1532–1611)

Master and Surveyor of the Ordnance in the North of England, 1570–1594; coalowner; founder of the Charterhouse

Engraving by Magdalena and Willem van de **Passe**. Illustration on p.127 of Henry Holland's *Herωologia* published in 1620.

(O'D 2; Hind: Part II, p.155, no. 35)

Thomas Sutton was born at Knaith in Lincolnshire in 1532, the son of Richard Sutton, steward of the courts in Lincoln. He is traditionally supposed to have been educated at Eton, later becoming a student of Lincoln's Inn. During the reign of Mary I, and for some years after her death, he travelled abroad, visiting Holland, France, Spain and Italy, possibly being engaged in military service.

He had friends among the nobility and appears to have served under men of rank as both secretary and soldier. He saw much service in the North of England and in 1570 was appointed Master and Surveyor of the Ordnance in the North. His last military duty was at the siege and capture of Edinburgh Castle in 1573.

Sutton's long experience in the North had made him aware of the rich coal deposits in County Durham and, in consequence, he secured leases on land owned by the Bishop of Durham and by the crown to enable him to undertake coal-mining activities there and to ship the coal to the lucrative London market. From this enterprise Sutton made a great fortune which was subsequently further augmented by his marriage in 1582 to Elizabeth Dudley, a wealthy widow of Stoke Newington, Middlesex.

Sutton transferred his business activities to London in 1580 and he continued to reside there and at his various houses in the environs of the city and in Essex and Cambridgeshire until his death. He was regarded by his contemporaries as the richest commoner in England, and it is perhaps significant of his commercial reputation that John Aubrey remarks that 'Twas from him that B Jonson took his hint of the fox, and by Signor Volpone is meant Sutton'. Whatever the truth of this comment Sutton announced in 1594 his major charitable intention of founding a hospital at Hallingbury Bouchers in Essex, making over various estates towards the intended foundation. In 1610 an Act of Parliament was passed to enable him to fulfil his promise. In the following year, however, he bought the Charterhouse property, situated to the north of the city of London, and was permitted to vary his intention and to establish a hospital and free school in the Charterhouse instead of at Hallingbury. In October 1611 he completed the endowment of his new foundation, allowing the exact form of the institution to be decided by the government. The establishment eventually fixed upon consisted of 80 pensioners and a school for 40 boys. The Charterhouse itself still remains on its original site although the school, greatly enlarged, was removed to Surrey in 1872.

Sutton did not long survive the birth of his new foundation, dying at his house at Hackney on 12 December 1611. His remains were subsequently buried in the chapel of the Charterhouse on the third anniversary of his death in 1614.

The right Honourable Sr Iulius
Cæsar knight, Mas ter of the Rowles,
and one of his Ma.ties most hon.ble serinie
Counsell.

R: Elstracke sculpsit

Are to be sold by Compton Holland ouer against theexchange

29   E.763–1960

29   Sir Julius Caesar (1558–1636)

Master of the Rolls

Engraving by Renold **Elstrack**.

(O'D 1; Hind: Part II, p.167, 7, 2nd state; R S, p.35 and plate 66)

The oddly-named Julius Caesar was of Italian extraction, his father, Cesare Adelmare, being a physician trained at the University of Padua who came to England and set up his practice in London about 1550, becoming, in turn, physician to both Queen Mary I and Queen Elizabeth. He was naturalized in 1558, the year of his celebrated son's birth, who, in due course, adopted Caesar as the family name, that being the name by which the doctor was known to his two royal patients.

Julius was educated at Magdalen Hall (later Magdalen College), Oxford, becoming BA in 1575 and MA in 1578. In the following year he travelled to Paris where in 1581 he took degrees in both civil and canon law at the university. In 1580 he became a member of the Inner Temple and subsequently secured various minor legal appointments. In 1584 he was made a judge in the Admiralty Court, a Master of Chancery and a Doctor of Laws in the University of Oxford.

In his work in the Admiralty Court he seems to have shown great generosity to many poor seamen and foreigners with whom he had dealings, apparently at considerable financial cost to himself. He became the senior member for Reigate in the Parliament of 1588 and eventually received a lucrative appointment as a master in the Court of Requests in 1591, in which year he also became a bencher of the Inner Temple. He was elected treasurer of his inn in 1593 and again in 1594. In 1592 he served in Parliament as the senior member for Bletchingley in Surrey. In due course he received various official appointments, the most valuable of which was the Mastership of St Katherine's Hospital by the Tower which came to him in 1596. In the following year he was again an MP, this time for Windsor.

He had become a close friend of Archbishop Whitgift and in 1598 received the direct favour of the queen who paid a visit to his house at Mitcham, stopping there overnight. At this time he became a considerable benefactor to the Inner Temple, making a generous contribution to the cost of new buildings. Throughout the remainder of his career he continued to aid his inn by his favour and interest as opportunity arose.

His successful progress continued and in 1600 he was appointed senior Master of Requests. In the following year he was again MP for Windsor and in 1603 was knighted by the new king. In 1606 he was appointed Chancellor of the Exchequer and Under-Treasurer, later being made a member of the Privy Council, and was deeply involved in the consideration of ways by which the king could raise additional money to meet his always pressing requirements.

In 1614 Caesar was again returned to Parliament, this time as senior member for Middlesex. In the autumn of that year he reached the climax of his career with his appointment as Master of the Rolls, surrendering his other offices of Chancellor of the Exchequer and Under-Treasurer.

His increasing prosperity was marked by

his purchase in 1615 from the 3rd Earl of Essex of an estate at Benington in Hertfordshire for which he paid a high price. In 1620 he was back in Parliament as senior member for Malden in Essex. That same year saw the disgrace of Francis Bacon, the Lord Chancellor (plate 30), and Caesar was appointed to hear Chancery cases from which the Chancellor had been barred and, later, to assist in arranging an accommodation between Bacon and his creditors. He appears to have acted as a sympathetic and generous friend to Bacon during the difficult circumstances of his removal from office and was later named by Bacon to serve as an executor of his will.

During his last years Sir Julius was concerned in an official enquiry into the Poor Law and with the reform of abuses in the Court of Chancery. He died on 18 April 1636 and was buried in the Church of Great St Helen's in Bishopsgate, where his father is also buried. He was three times married and had eight children by his first two wives. His third wife, whom he married in 1615, was niece to Francis Bacon.

Whilst not regarded by his contemporaries as possessing a great legal mind, Caesar was esteemed and respected for his freedom from corruption and for his many acts of charity. A contemporary described him as 'A person of prodigious bounty to all of worth or want, so that he might seem to be almoner-general of the nation'.

30 E.3061–1960

30 Francis Bacon, Viscount St Albans (1561–1626)

Lord Chancellor, philosopher and essayist

Engraving by Crispin van de **Passe II**, after an engraving by Simon van de **Passe** based on a painting by William **Larkin**.

(O'D 22; Hind: Part II, p.250; R S, p.13)

Francis Bacon was born at York House in London on 22 January 1561, the son of Sir Nicholas Bacon, the Lord Keeper, and his wife Ann Cooke, daughter of Sir Anthony Cooke. He entered Trinity College, Cambridge, in April 1573 and remained there until March 1575. He was admitted as a student at Gray's Inn in June 1576.

In 1576 he accompanied an embassy to France and was still abroad when his father died in February 1579. He resumed his legal studies and was admitted as a barrister in June 1582, sitting for the borough of Melcombe Regis in Dorset in the Parliament of 1584. He composed at this time a memoir of political advice, addressed to the queen, which foreshadows his later subtle and sophisticated modes of thought. In the Parliament of 1586 he sat for Taunton and in the same year was elected a bencher of Gray's Inn. In the Parliament of 1589 he sat for Liverpool and by then had an assured position in the House of Commons, serving on numerous committees.

Although nephew by marriage to Lord Burghley (plate 13) he secured little influence through the relationship, and in 1591 began his friendship with the young Earl of Essex (plate 18) through whom he hoped to exert personal influence on political events in England. In the Parliament of 1593 he sat for Middlesex and led opposition to the granting of higher taxes demanded by the Lords on the queen's behalf. This displeased the queen and he failed to become either Attorney-General or Solicitor-General as he had hoped. Essex expressed his confidence in Bacon by a gift of land, but in 1595 Bacon was expressing a wish to withdraw from both politics and the law in order to devote himself to philosophy. He busied himself with the preparation for publication of his celebrated *Essays*, which were issued in 1597. He was by then in financial trouble and sought to make a rich marriage and secure a lucrative office but both projects failed.

He was again in Parliament in 1597, this time sitting for Southampton, and at the close of September he was briefly arrested for debt. His efforts to interest Essex in the problems of governing Ireland failed, for Essex quarrelled with the queen and by the time this was resolved Ireland was in revolt. Essex proved a complete disaster as commander in Ireland and his foolhardiness in abandoning his post and returning to court posed great problems for Bacon in his attempts to be loyal to both the queen and Essex. Inevitably he managed to offend both. Essex's discontent led him to the attempted revolt of February 1601 and Bacon then found himself, as one of the most prominent lawyers of the day, taking a leading part in the prosecution of the earl for treason. There is, however, no room for doubt that Bacon was fully convinced of Essex's treason and totally sincere in his condemnation of his former patron.

On the accession of James I Bacon hoped for early preferment but little came his way.

He was, however, knighted along with many others in July 1603. In the new Parliament of 1604 Bacon sat for Ipswich. He hoped to see put into effect some of his proposals for greater religious tolerance, for effecting the political union with Scotland and for bringing about a better relationship between the new king and the House of Commons, but without any success. He was one of the commissioners to consider the terms of union with Scotland but their proposals were not brought before the House until 1606, Gunpowder Plot intervening, and Bacon turned his mind to the completion and publication in October 1605 of his book *Advancement of Learning*, which is, in effect, a major review of the current state of knowledge.

On 10 May 1606 Bacon married Alice Barnham, daughter and heiress of a former Sheriff of London. From November 1606 Parliament was absorbed in discussion of the proposals for union with Scotland, with Bacon as the principal advocate of the scheme. He made a notable speech in support of the proposals on 17 February 1607 but failed to secure the assent of the Commons. Soon afterwards, however, he received his long-hoped-for promotion when, on 25 June 1607, he at last became Solicitor-General. This brought no increase in political influence, for Lord Treasurer Salisbury (formerly Sir Robert Cecil) blocked his means of access to the king. He continued with his philosophical and other writings, publishing in 1608 his work on the wisdom of the ancients *De Sapientis Veterum*.

By 1611 the king and Salisbury had failed to secure agreement with the Commons on the urgent problem of raising revenue and Parliament was dismissed in an atmosphere of general bad feeling. Bacon realized that he

had no chance of political influence while Salisbury was alive but on the latter's death in 1612 Bacon approached the king to offer his political services. There was no immediate response in terms of office but he did receive permission to write to the king on matters of state. He was thus able to communicate to the king his ideas on the problems of raising adequate revenue while maintaining an harmonious relationship between king and Parliament. There seems little doubt that if his ideas had been adopted the evils of the next half-century might have been averted.

In October 1613 he was appointed Attorney-General and in the Parliament of 1614 he represented the University of Cambridge. The session ended in a renewed quarrel between king and Commons. While Bacon supported the instinct of the king towards absolutism he also wished James to maintain, if possible, a friendly relationship with Parliament and was dismayed that each session should dissolve into an acrid squabble over money supplies.

At the trial of the Earl and Countess of Somerset in May 1616 for the murder of Sir Thomas Overbury, Bacon appeared as chief prosecutor and secured convictions, although the king was later to pardon both offenders. Bacon now hoped to pursue his political aims through the king's new favourite, George Villiers (later Duke of Buckingham). He was promised succession to the office of Lord Chancellor as soon as Lord Ellesmere, the ailing incumbent, died. A long-standing dispute between Lord Justice Coke and Bacon over the independence of the judiciary was coming to a head, a dispute which resulted in the dismissal of Coke in November 1616. Bacon had, meanwhile, been appointed to the

Privy Council in June 1616 and was made Lord Keeper on the death of Ellesmere in March 1617. He was subsequently made Lord Chancellor in January 1618 and was then created Baron Verulam.

Bacon displayed great energy in his new office, speedily clearing all arrears of business in the Court of Chancery and his judicial conduct seems to have been exemplary. He was, however, subjected to constant pressure from Buckingham to show favour to certain litigants. He was closely concerned with the trials of Ralegh (plate 34) in 1618, of the Earl of Suffolk in 1619 and of the Attorney-General, Sir Henry Yelverton, in 1620. In January 1621 he was promoted in the peerage and created Viscount St Albans. His great work entitled *Novum Organum* was published in October 1620. This was an attempt to construct a new system of philosophy based on inductive reasoning as opposed to the deductive reasoning derived from the philosophy of Aristotle. Although incomplete the book was to have a great influence on the development of logic, philosophy and science.

The new Parliament assembled at the end of January 1621 and it was apparent that there was now considerable feeling directed against Bacon in his capacity as the king's minister and as one who had recommended the granting of certain monopolies of great financial benefit to the hated Buckingham. Opposition to Bacon grew and opportunity was taken to make two unusual complaints against his judicial conduct, it being alleged that he had taken gifts of money from litigants and then decided the cases in question against those who had paid the money. Bacon himself wrote at this time that 'I know I have clean hands and a clean heart' and it is reasonable to assume

that this was indeed so, given the current practice of judges accepting presents from litigants at the close of a case. However, it was clear that Bacon had accepted presents while cases were pending, although there is no evidence that such gifts affected his final judgment. When the House of Lords began to examine the charges Bacon made no defence and confessed to his lack of propriety in those matters. He was deprived of the Great Seal on 1 May 1621 and was subsequently fined £40,000, briefly committed to the Tower and forbidden to attend Parliament or to be present at court. The king tempered the severity of the sentence by entrusting the fine to trustees to be administered for Bacon's own use and by issuing a pardon to protect him from other demands. Early in 1622 Bacon was also able to obtain a relaxation of the prohibition against coming near the court. His official career in ruins he turned again to his writings and in October 1621 completed his valuable *History of Henry VII* and then moved on to the expansion, completion and translation into Latin of his *Advancement of Learning* which eventually appeared in 1623 under the title of *De Augmentis Scientiarum*. He also embarked on his long-contemplated digest of the laws of England.

The death of the king and the accession of Charles I in March 1625 in no way mitigated the ban on his political activities. He continued to work on his philosophical writings but gradually his health began to fail. In March 1626 he left his coach when travelling near Highgate in order to collect snow to carry out an experiment of stuffing a chicken with it in order to observe the preservative effect of the cold. He caught a chill, however, and died of bronchitis on 9 April. He was

buried in St Michael's Church, St Albans.

Although his political career ended in failure and disgrace Bacon, through his writings, was a reformer of scientific method of major significance. He was concerned to propagate the practice of the inductive method in philosophy. His new system was to be applicable not only to natural philosophy but to all sciences, indeed to the whole world of knowledge. Bacon enjoined a regular scientific method employing a logical chain of demonstrative reasoning which insisted on the importance of experiment as well as observation. His future influence was such that Macaulay was able to say of him that he 'moved the intellects which moved the world'.

A commentator remembering Bacon in 1653 describes him as being 'of middling stature, his countenance had indented with age before he was old; his presence grave and comely'. It should be noted that the engraver of this portrait made a mistake in depicting the seal bag held by Bacon, as it carries the name of Charles I rather than that of James I.

CONCILIVM SEPTEM NOBILIVM ANGLORVM CONIVRANTIVM IN NECEM IACOBI · I ·
MAGNAE BRITANNIAE REGIS TOTIVSQ· ANGLICI CONVOCATI PARLEMENTI

Robert Winter
Bates
Christopher Wright
John Wright
Thomas Percy
Guido Fawkes
Robert Catesby
Thomas Winter

Vides Spectator humanissime .hic expressas effigies septem Anglorum qui Regem suum cum praecipuis Status Anglici Proceribus ad Parlementum, ut vocant comvocatis pulvere tormentario simul horrendo modo in ipsa domo Parlementi evertere voluerunt. Cuius Coniurationis nefandae Auctores fuere inprimis Robertus Catesby et Thomas Perci, qui sibi denui adiunxere alios, Videlicet. Thomam et Robertum Winter, Guidonem Fawkens Iohannem et Christopherium Wright quibus demum accessit Bates Roberti Catesbi Famulus. Sed coniuratione hac Diuina prouidentia et clementia decem aut viuis horas ante futura Cessurum Parlamenti Detecta. et Coniuratis persecutis ex iis Robertus Catesbi et Thomas Perci ictu sclopeti periere et eorum Capita domui Parlamenti inperpetuam rei memoriam imposita caeteri, cum multis aliis qui eandem in rem conspirarunt adhuc captui detinentur. dignam facinore sententiam expectantes.

Icy se voient les effigies des sept Seigneurs Anglois lesquels de façon nouuelle et fort Horrible on attente contre le Roy et son estat aians entrepins p mines et quantite de puldre de faire Saillir sa Maies te auec les premiers Du Royaulme et principaux officiers estans en parlement a Westmuns ter les premiers auteurs de la diste coniuration Sont, Robert Catesby et Thomas Percij, auxquels depuis adioinct es Thomas et Robert Winter, Guido Fawkes Iean et Christophe Wright, et depuis encor le Seruiteur dudit Catesby appelle Bates Mais estante ladist Conspiration decouuerte p la grace et prouidence de Dieu, enuiron dix heures deuant lassemble et assiette dudist parlement et les distes Conspirateurs poursuiuis lesdis premiers auteurs Catesby et Percy sont es te attamctis et tues de Harquebusade leurs tes tes coupees et portees a Westmunster et posees la maison du parlement en memoire de l'acte det Fable Restans auec plusieurs auitres trouues Coulpables dudist fauct sont encor prisonniers, attendans larrest du Parlement condigne a leurs merites.

Hie habt ihr gunstiger Leser etliche nemlich, der furnemsten Engellander, Welche ohnlangst ihren König sampt dem gantzen Parlament mit Buchsen pulfer schrocklicher Weijs zuvertilgen furgenommen nach dem leben abgebildet, vnd sind diese: Robert Catesby vnd Thomas Percy so noch andere hernach zu sich gezogen, nemlich Thomas vnd Robert Winter Guido Fawkes Iohn vnd Christopher Wright, neben Bates Catesbys Diener, nachdem aber die Verrahterey entdeckt, sind Ro Catesby vnd Percy vondenen so sie verfolgt erschosse. Aihre Heupter auff das Parlaments hauss gesetzt worden: die andere aber so noch gefahr habe noch ihre verdiente lohn zuerwarten.

31 E.3980–1960

31 The Gunpowder Plot Conspirators

Engraving possibly by Crispin van de **Passe I**.

(O'D, Groups 2; Hind: Part II, p.391, 64)

The Gunpowder Plot was a conspiracy by a small group of Roman Catholic gentlemen to assassinate King James I and the members of the two Houses of Parliament when the king came to open a session of Parliament. It had been begun early in 1604 as a response to the new king's recent intensification of the severe Elizabethan penal laws against Catholics and as an attempt to end the Protestant supremacy in England.

Although Guy Fawkes is the best remembered of the conspirators he was not one of the original small group of plotters, which consisted of Robert Catesby, John Wright and Thomas Winter. Fawkes was known as a man of great courage, having recently served with distinction in the Spanish army in Europe, and was brought into the plot at an early stage along with Thomas Percy.

By May 1604 Percy managed to hire a building adjacent to Parliament where Fawkes was put in charge, he being little known in England. The original intention of mining beneath the House of Lords was abandoned when, after delays in summoning Parliament, it became possible for the plotters to hire a cellar located directly beneath the House of Lords. This they proceeded to fill with barrels of gunpowder. All was ready by May 1605 but the meeting of Parliament had by then been deferred to the autumn. However, the number of conspirators had been enlarged to include Winter's brother Robert, Wright's brother Christopher, Robert Keyes, John Grant and Catesby's servant, Thomas Bates, and about Michaelmas 1605 three wealthy country gentlemen, Sir Everard Digby, Francis Tresham and Ambrose Rookwood were also recruited. The last were expected to instigate an armed rising in the Midlands once the king and Parliament had been destroyed. In addition several Jesuit priests may have become aware of the plot, including Father Henry Garnett (plate 43). The long delay and the increasing number of those involved in the plot proved fatal. It had been decided that no warning should be given to Catholic peers but Francis Tresham sent on 26 October an ambiguous letter of warning to his brother-in-law, Lord Monteagle, which the latter immediately took to Lord Salisbury, the Lord Treasurer. By 31 October the character of the plot was understood at court but the authorities decided to bide their time. Fawkes with great coolness and courage remained at his post and was finally arrested during the night of 4 November. The other plotters fled and Fawkes was tortured. He revealed nothing for several days, although by then several of the men involved were already dead or arrested. Catesby, Percy and the two Wrights were killed at Holbeach House, near Stourbridge, and the remainder were executed, with the exception of Tresham who died in the Tower. Father Garnett was also seized and executed.

It is improbable that the portraits contained in this print are accurate. Indeed it is difficult to see how the subjects of a print of this character, made in Utrecht, could be other than generalized. Nevertheless, it remains a powerful contemporary evocation of the principal conspirators and the descriptions of the plot in Latin, French and German which it

bears show the enormous interest aroused in Europe by the attempted coup.

32   Sir Martin Frobisher (1535?–1594)

Navigator

Engraving by Magdalena and Willem van de **Passe**. Illustration to face p.97 of Henry Holland's *Heroologia* published in 1620.

(O'D 2; Hind: Part I, p.155, 27)

Martin Frobisher was born at Altofts, near Normanton, in Yorkshire, but on the death of his father the child was sent to London to live with relatives. When old enough he was sent to sea and made his first voyage to Guinea, on the south-west coast of Africa, in 1554, making further annual voyages to either North Africa or the Middle East during the next decade.

In 1566 he was noted in official papers as being suspected of involvement in piracy, but by 1571 he was in state employment in a vessel serving off the coast of Ireland. Through various services he became known to Sir Humphrey Gilbert who, with the queen's approval, was then much concerned with the possibility of discovering a north-west sea passage to China. The responsibility for organizing such an expedition fell to the Muscovy Company which commissioned Frobisher in February 1575 to undertake the first of his voyages on its behalf.

He sailed from the Thames with three small

FORBISHERUS euans NEPTUNIA regna frequentat
Pro patria at tandem glande peremplus obit

32   E.3083–1960

vessels in June 1576, proceeding up the North Sea and past the Shetland and Faroe Islands to Cape Farewell at the southern tip of Greenland. In a storm the vessels became separated, the smallest was lost and the second returned to England, leaving Frobisher to sail on alone to Labrador and Baffin Island. He returned to Harwich on 2 October 1576 with sealskins, bearskins and a specimen of black pyrite ore which an alchemist claimed contained gold, although the London goldsmiths denied the suggestion. The prospect of very large profits hastened the preparations for a second voyage, which was primarily intended as a quest for gold rather than for the North-West Passage. A new company, the Company of Cathay, was formed in March 1577 and a fleet of three vessels sailed from the Thames on 27 May 1577 to the same area as had been explored in the previous year and in September brought back to Milford Haven about 200 tons of the supposed gold-bearing ore. The ore proved to be valueless but the self-deceiving avarice of those backing the new company was such that it was resolved to despatch yet another and larger expedition in the following year. Accordingly, Frobisher set out from Harwich on 31 May 1578 in command of a fleet of 15 vessels. After dispersal by bad weather the fleet lost much time in re-assembling at the point of rendezvous and those still sound enough were loaded with the worthless ore and made their way back to England, arriving at various ports in the early part of October. The results of attempts to refine the ore were as disappointing as previously and Frobisher found himself in disfavour and his family in grave financial difficulties.

By 1580 he had so far recovered his position as to be in command of one of the queen's ships patrolling against the Spaniards off the southern coast of Ireland. In 1582 when a fourth expedition to the North-West was fitted out Frobisher was again to have had command but he wisely withdrew from the project. In September 1585 he sailed from Plymouth as Drake's vice-admiral in command of the *Primrose* in the expedition to the West Indies. He served with distinction in the attack upon Cartagena and returned safely to England in July 1586.

In the action against the Armada in July 1588 Frobisher was in command of the *Triumph* and initially joined with Drake and Sir John Hawkins in defeating the Spanish rear-admiral and another great ship on 21–22 July. Three days later he was in command of a newly-formed squadron and on 29 July, again with Drake and Hawkins, he assisted in the final defeat of the Spaniards off Gravelines. A few days earlier he had been knighted at sea by the Lord High Admiral, Lord Howard of Effingham (plate 15). In November he was in command of a squadron patrolling the Narrow Seas and in May 1589 was in action off Ostend. In May of the following year he served as vice-admiral to Hawkins with a fleet of 12 or 14 ships intended to intercept the Portuguese fleet coming from India, but this project failed to succeed.

Frobisher clearly cherished his Yorkshire origins for in the summer of 1591, when he married for the second time, he was living at Whitwood, very close to his birthplace at Altofts, and in 1593 he was again in Yorkshire, being then appointed a Justice of the Peace.

In May 1592 he was at sea serving off the coast of Spain, where he captured a vessel with a valuable cargo. In the autumn of 1594, however, he set off on what was to prove to be his last voyage. A fleet of 11 ships was sent to attempt the relief of Brest and Crozon, which were in the hands of the Spaniards. Frobisher was wounded in the fight which led to the garrison's surrender and the destruction of the fort, and inexpert medical attention led to his death soon after his return to Plymouth. His entrails were buried in St Andrew's Church in that city and his other remains were buried in London at St Giles' Church, Cripplegate, on 14 January 1595.

There is no evidence concerning the source of this portrait, which appears to show Frobisher at about the age of 50.

33 Sir Francis Drake (1540?–1596)

Circumnavigator and admiral

Engraving by Thomas de **Leu** after a portrait by Jean **Rabel,** based in turn on an engraving by Jodocus **Hondius** made about 1583 and stated to be taken from life.

(O'D 2; R S, p.71)

Drake, the most famous navigator and naval commander of his day, was born near Tavistock about 1540. Little is known of his early years but he seems to have been apprenticed to the master of a small sailing vessel. He took part in voyages to Guinea and the Spanish Main in 1565–66 and in John Hawkins' ill-fated expedition destroyed by the Spaniards in 1568. Drake's ship and one other were the only survivors and he was called on to make a personal report to Cecil, the queen's great

Habes Lector candide fortiſſ, ac inuictiſſ. Ducis Draeck ad viuum Jmaginem qui toto terrarum orbe, duorum annorum, et menſium decem ſpatio, Zephiris fauentibus circumducto Angliam ſedes proprias, 4. Cal. Octobr̃ anno a partu virginis 1580 reuiſit cum antea portu ſoluiſſet Jd. Decembr̃ anni 1577.

Le vray portraict du Cappitaine Draeck lequel a circuit toute la terre en trois annees moins deux mois et 17 iours il partit du Royaulme D'Angleterre le 17 de Decembre 1577 et fist ſon retour audict Royaulme le 26. iour de Sept: 1580.

Ad Ampliſſimum et Illuſt: virum D.D. Edoardum Staffart apud Henricum 3. Chryſt: Francæ Regem legatum D.S. Obſeruantiſs.

Jo. Rabel Pinxit.   Thomas de leu ſculpſit et excudit.

minister (plate 13), thus first attracting royal interest. He subsequently made voyages to Guinea and the West Indies in 1570, 1571 and 1572. From this last voyage he returned to Plymouth in triumph in August 1573 with considerable treasure and then served in Ireland with the Earl of Essex (plate 18) until 1576.

On returning to Plymouth from Ireland he fitted out five ships, including his own ship the *Pelican* (later renamed the *Golden Hind*), which sailed for Brazil in December 1577. Three of the ships then sailed south from there to the Straits of Magellan, but only two survived the passage of the straits in August 1578 and these were then separated by storms. Drake sailed on alone up the coast of South America, capturing a great treasure ship near Callao on 1 March 1579 and afterwards continuing to sail further up the coast, apparently as far as San Francisco Bay. From there he sailed for 68 days across the Pacific, eventually passing through the Indian Archipelago and on to the Cape of Good Hope which he passed on 15 June 1580. He finally reached Plymouth again on 26 September 1580, having taken just over two years and nine months to complete the first English circumnavigation of the globe. The queen accepted the major part of the treasure Drake had seized and honoured him with a knighthood in April 1581.

In 1582 he was mayor of Plymouth and in 1584-85 the MP for Bossiney. In 1585 he was back at sea commanding an expedition against the West Indies which, after doing great damage, eventually reached Virginia and brought the disheartened original settlers home to England.

Spain's preparations for war against England were increasing and in response to the threat Drake commanded a strong expedition in April 1587 which succeeded in destroying 33 Spanish ships at Cadiz and in causing further great damage to shipping. On his return he urged on the queen the need for a continuing aggressive policy against Spain, but she was unwilling to agree and the Armada eventually sailed against England from Corunna on 12 July 1588. The Spaniards were sighted off the Lizard on 20 July and were pursued from Plymouth by the English fleet. The smaller, better-armed and better-manned English ships had the advantage in manoeuvre and attack over the larger, more cumbersome Spanish vessels, with the result that the Armada was harried up the Channel for some days and then attacked off Calais by Drake's fireships on the night of 28 July. On the following day the decisive action was fought off Gravelines which ended with the surviving Spanish ships in flight northwards. Drake's further action against the Spanish and Portuguese coasts in April 1589 ended all possibility of any further Spanish invasion attempt against England. Back at home Drake demonstrated energy and drive on shore. He provided Plymouth with a water supply in 1591, built mills on his own behalf and was again MP for Plymouth in the Parliament of 1593. In the following year the queen ordered him to take command of another expedition to the West Indies. This time, however, because of delays, the Spaniards became aware of the projected attack and prepared to resist it. The expedition sailed in August 1595. At Puerto Rico the vice-admiral, Sir John Hawkins, died just before the attack, Sir Nicholas Clifford, the military commander, was killed by a stray shot and the English attack was finally beaten off. The ships went on to burn various ports, but these were found to be abandoned and empty of treasure. Drake fell ill with dysentery and died off Portobello on 28 January 1596, being buried at sea the following day.

John Stow described Drake as being 'low of stature, of strong limbs, broad breasted, round headed, brown hair, full bearded; his eyes round, large and clear; well favoured, fair, and of a cheerful countenance'. The portrait is believed to be an authentic representation of him at the age of 43.

34   Sir Walter Ralegh (1552?–1618)

Military and naval commander, explorer and author

Engraving by Simon van de **Passe** based on an unknown source. Frontispiece to the third edition (1617) of Ralegh's *History of the World*.

(O'D 21; Hind: Part II, p.266, 48, 2nd state; R S, p.259, plate 507)

Walter Ralegh was the son of a Protestant country gentleman of the same name who had an estate at Hayes, near Budleigh Salterton, in Devon. He was born about 1552 to his father's third wife, who had previously been married to Otho Gilbert and whose son Humphrey, later the celebrated navigator, was thus half-brother to Ralegh. The sea-going tradition was clearly strong in the family for Ralegh appears with his elder brother, his half-brother Humphrey Gilbert and other half-brothers in a list of sea-captains drawn up in 1585 at the

34   E.3100–1960

time of a rumoured impending Spanish invasion of England. He appears to have been educated locally, later proceeding to Oriel College, Oxford, where the length of his stay is uncertain.

In 1569 he was serving in France in the Huguenot cause. He is known to have been in London in 1576 and 1577 and may have served as a soldier in the Low Countries in 1577 or 1578. In the latter part of 1578 he was engaged with his elder brother Carew and with Humphrey Gilbert in a profitless voyage to the Azores or the West Indies. Soon afterwards, however, he was at court on terms of friendship with the Earl of Leicester and becoming notorious for his brawling disposition. In June 1580 he sailed for Ireland in command of a company of soldiers and saw much violent service there, including being responsible for the killing of 600 surrendered Spanish and Italian adventurers.

In December 1581 he was back at court with despatches from Ireland and while there he attracted the notice of the queen, speedily becoming a favourite, so that within a few years, through the bestowal of various grants and offices, he became a very wealthy man. In 1594 he was knighted and he sat in the Parliaments of both 1585 and 1586. In 1586 he was granted vast estates in Ireland and made captain of the queen's guard and in the following year he received the estates forfeited by the Babington conspirators.

In 1584 Ralegh was granted a patent authorizing him to seek new lands and to hold them in the queen's name. An expedition despatched by him in April 1584 explored the American seaboard from Florida northwards, eventually claiming jurisdiction over that whole area from Florida to Newfoundland originally named Virginia. His agents established a colony in 1585 which was evacuated by Drake in the following year. Another colony established in 1587 had disappeared completely by the time relief appeared in 1589. The queen's insistence that Ralegh should remain at court meant that he himself was never able to make the voyage to Virginia. After vast expenditure he was obliged to abandon the scheme, although further efforts to renew it were made in subsequent years. This was, however, the first attempt to establish English colonies overseas and, therefore, very significant for future developments. Two immediate consequences of the voyages were that tobacco and the potato were both introduced into England by about 1586 and Ralegh is known to have begun the cultivation of the potato on his own lands in Ireland.

In 1588 Ralegh was a member of a commission concerned with the land defences of England against possible Spanish invasion and it is unlikely that he took any part in the naval action against the Armada. By the end of the year he was again at court and in dispute with the queen's new favourite, the Earl of Essex (plate 18). In 1589 he was much in Ireland, returning to court in October and bringing with him his friend the poet Edmund Spenser, who was well received by the queen. Ralegh did not stay long at court, however, as the jealousy of Essex and his friends was troublesome to him. He withdrew to pursue his official duties and his private interests in the West Country.

In 1591 Ralegh sought a command in an expedition to the West Indies but once again the queen refused to let him go. The following year found him fitting out an even stronger force with himself in command despite the queen's unwillingness. He promised her that he would return before the completion of the full expedition and finally sailed despite receiving an urgent recall. He succeeded in capturing a great treasure-ship off the Azores and fulfilled his promise by returning to his London house at the beginning of June. In the following month he was committed to the Tower, having seriously angered the queen by his liaison with Elizabeth Throgmorton, one of her maids of honour, an intrigue discovered just before he set sail and the reason for his recall. The unfortunate lady was also conveyed to the Tower and there they both remained until the captured treasure-ship reached Dartmouth. Ralegh – still under arrest – was sent down with Cecil and Drake to supervise the landing of the treasure and to prevent pillage of the vessel. The queen was delighted with her share – the major part – of the booty and eventually relented towards Ralegh, setting both him and his lady free. They appear to have married at once and retired to Sherborne Castle in Dorset, which Ralegh had recently acquired, where they began an extensive programme of renovation. He was member for a Cornish seat in the Parliament of 1593 and thus back in London. At his house in the Strand he mixed freely with philosophers and men of letters, indulging in free discussions on religion which brought him into disrepute. The atheist playwright Christopher Marlowe was a member of this group and Ralegh came under some suspicion of heresy after the order by the Privy Council for Marlowe's arrest and his subsequent murder in 1593.

In February 1595 Ralegh sailed from Plymouth with five ships in search of the fabled gold of El Dorado. He captured the island of Trinidad and gained information from its Spanish governor which enabled him to set off for the Orinoco river. With a small expeditionary force and five small ships he proceeded up the river for 400 or 500 miles, but without making any significant discovery other than specimens of gold-bearing ores. He returned to England in August where there was now sufficient malice against him to cause his account of the voyage to be disbelieved. In justification he wrote his celebrated *Discoverie of Guiana*, published in 1596, a full and largely accurate account of the central area of Venezuela.

On his return Ralegh, as Lord-Lieutenant of Cornwall, concerned himself with matters of defence because of the supposed threat of a new Spanish invasion attempt and these duties prevented him from undertaking another voyage to Guiana in 1596. In June of that year he played a brilliant role in the expedition against Cadiz commanded by Lord Howard of Effingham, the Lord Admiral (plate 15), and the Earl of Essex. Having made fruitless efforts to gain further information about the Orinoco and its mines he finally abandoned his project, only reviving it in a time of dire necessity 20 years later.

By May 1597 Ralegh was back at court and apparently again in the queen's favour as well as being on good terms with Essex. The queen accepted Ralegh's argument that the best way to deal with the Spanish threat was by attack. Accordingly a fleet put to sea in July under the command of Essex, with Ralegh as his vice-admiral. It suffered setbacks due to bad weather and by the time it was assembled in the Azores Essex had determined to sail on to Madeira, hoping to stand a better chance of encountering the Spanish treasure fleet. Ralegh was to join Essex there but as things turned out he arrived first and proceeded to capture the town of Fayal, to the intense anger of Essex when he got there. His chagrin was such that the relations between the two men were permanently soured.

The years following were spent between the court, the West Country and Ireland. Ralegh served in the Parliaments of 1597 and 1601 and in September 1600 was made Governor of Jersey, behaving subsequently with his usual energy and effectiveness in the affairs of the island. However, he was subject to Essex's active jealousy and he and his partisans lost no chance of attacking Ralegh verbally and, on at least one occasion, physically. This bitterness was only ended by the execution of Essex in 1601.

With the accession of James I Ralegh's position became precarious, for his enemies – who were numerous – had systematically poisoned the king's mind against him. He was deprived successively of his offices of Captain of the Guard, Warden of the Stannaries and Governor of Jersey. He was also deprived of his valuable wine licences monopoly and obliged to vacate his town residence in the Strand. Finally, in July 1603, he was accused of complicity in the plots against the king hatched by his friend Lord Cobham and the latter's associate William Weston. He was committed to the Tower and in November was put on trial at Winchester before a special commission, largely composed of his enemies, and was inevitably found guilty of treason. His execution was fixed for 11 December and Ralegh fully expected to die. However, on the day before, the king reprieved Ralegh and Cobham and both were sent to the Tower. All his offices and estates were forfeited to the crown, but arrangements were made to supply Lady Ralegh and his family with an income. They came to live with him in the Tower where he was kept in fairly lenient conditions. A friendship developed between Henry, Prince of Wales (plate 11), and Ralegh, largely due to the prince's interest in literature and scientific studies, and he began to write for the prince his celebrated *History of the World*. He was also allowed special facilities to conduct scientific experiments. By 1610 he felt sufficiently secure to propose that he should be released to undertake another voyage to the Orinoco to look for gold and silver mines. His proposal was given serious consideration and he was eventually released in March 1616.

Ralegh immediately set about preparations for his voyage with the assistance of loyal friends and relatives, but money was difficult to procure and no adequately trained or experienced crews could be found. The Spanish ambassador protested at the proposed expedition on the grounds that the lands in question were claimed by Spain, that England and Spain were at peace and that the expedition could lead to piracy against the Mexican plate fleet. Despite Ralegh's denials it seems that piracy was very much in mind as well as the proposed exploration. The fleet of 14 ships sailed in June 1617 but circumstances conspired against Ralegh. The weather was adverse, one of the ships sank, the voyage across the Atlantic was delayed and then proved difficult, for the fleet was first buffeted by hurricanes and then becalmed for 40 days while fever and scurvy took their toll. Many officers and men died and the crews became mutinous. However, at the mouth of the Cayenne river Ralegh was well received by friendly Indians and his ships (now reduced to 10) were able to recover after the hazardous crossing. The five smallest ships were chosen for the voyage up the Orinoco, while the remainder – commanded by Ralegh who was weakened by fever – remained at the coast to deal with any Spanish threat. The force moving up the river was obliged to attack and burn the Spanish settlement of San Tomas, an action in which Ralegh's son Walter was killed. The Spaniards succeeded in preventing the English from moving in the direction of the mines and they were eventually obliged to withdraw. Ralegh was grief-stricken at the death of his son and chagrined at the failure of the expedition. He desired to make another attempt but his disheartened men refused to follow him. They also refused to go in search of the Mexican plate fleet. The English fleet broke up with Ralegh going north to Newfoundland with four ships but, finding the crews unwilling to look for prizes, he finally set out for England and whatever fate had in store for him, arriving at Plymouth in June 1618.

The Spanish ambassador had already protested against the attack on San Tomas and had demanded that Ralegh and any others responsible should be surrendered to Spain for execution. Ralegh was arrested soon after his arrival and kept at Plymouth for some time before being brought to London. Both in Plymouth and in London he had opportunities for escape but left it too late. His eventual attempt to escape to France failed and he was captured and returned to the Tower. A commission of enquiry into Ralegh's actions was set up under the presidency of Francis Bacon, the Lord Chancellor (plate 30). The commission was conducted conscientiously but found itself confused and irritated by Ralegh's lies and prevarications, eventually concluding that the mine or mines had, in fact, never existed and that the king had been the victim of a deliberate deceit. The king wished Ralegh to be tried but was told that such a course was impossible as he was already under sentence of death from his earlier trial in 1603. On 29 October 1618 he was executed at Westminster, his body being interred in St Margaret's Church. His head was embalmed and retained by his widow until her death in 1647.

Ralegh was a handsome, vain man who made many enemies who did not fail to point out his major character defects such as pride, covetousness and unscrupulous dealing. He was also, however, a devoted English patriot possessing an imperial vision and great physical courage, who eventually came to be regarded as an archetypal defender of England against Spanish aggression who had been unjustly convicted in 1603 and basely put to death in 1618. His literary reputation is based on very solid achievements, despite the fact that much of both his poetry and prose has been lost. He published during his lifetime *A Report of the Truth of the Fight about the Isles of Azores*, London, 1591, the *Discoverie of the Empyre of Guiana*, London, 1596, and his *History of the Worlde*, London, 1614 (this last work being but the first part, ending in 130 BC, of an intended three-part history to be written for Henry, Prince of Wales, who died in 1612). Other minor writings continued to be published throughout and beyond the century following his execution.

The present portrait is the only one known to have been made during his period of confinement in the Tower.

Aemulus æquorei, admiratorque Draconis
Commodiore via, et ſpacijs breuioribus Orbem
Circumagens, patriam multa cum laude reuiſi;
Pluraque Neptuno et digniſſima Marte peregi.
Si Mare Cretensis nescit, tum nesciet Anglus
Oceanum, et t'uiet poſitis inglorius armis.

35 E.2986–1960

35 Thomas Cavendish (1560–1592)

Circumnavigator

Engraving by Crispin van de **Passe I** after an engraving by Jodocus **Hondius.** Illustration to C. van de Passe's *Effigies Regum Ac Principum . . .* , Cologne, 1598.

(O'D 5; Hind: Part II, p.39, 1.4)

Thomas Cavendish (a variant spelling of the name, Candish, is used on the engraving) was born at his family home, Grimston Hall, Trimley St Martin, near Harwich, in Suffolk, being baptized on 19 September 1560. Little is known of his youth and it is assumed that lack of money brought him – like other impoverished gentlemen – to a life of piracy.

He took his own ship on Sir Richard Grenville's expedition to colonize Virginia in 1585, a voyage which yielded great plunder from the Spaniards. On his return to England in September 1585 Cavendish immediately began to plan his own expedition to emulate Drake's circumnavigation of the globe eight years earlier. This voyage, undertaken by three ships under Cavendish's command, is fully documented in two separate accounts. They set sail from Plymouth on 21 July 1586 and voyaged via the Canaries to Sierra Leone. From there the passage across the Atlantic to South America began on 6 September and they arrived off the coast of Brazil on 31 October. After re-fitting they sailed southwards at the end of November to the Straits of Magellan. The hazardous voyage through the straits took more than six weeks in

January and February 1587. The ships then sailed on up the Pacific coast, attacking Spanish shipping and looting as opportunity arose. Near the Equator the smallest ship was deliberately sunk because loss of men made it impossible to provide a crew. From the pilot of a ship captured off the coast of Guatemala early in July Cavendish learned that a great treasure-ship was on its way from the Philippines. His two ships continued to sail on up to Mexico and from mid-October to mid-November patrolled the coast. Their patience was rewarded, for on 14 November they sighted and captured the King of Spain's great ship, the *Great St Anna*, laden with a large sum in gold coins and much valuable cargo. Cavendish and his men took what they could and burned the rest. On 19 November Cavendish set sail across the Pacific, heading for England, leaving behind his second ship, which was never seen again.

In his own vessel, the *Desire*, he made the difficult navigation of the Philippines and the Moluccas, eventually reaching Java in safety. He sailed on across the Indian Ocean to Africa, sighting the Cape of Good Hope on 19 March 1588. He was at St Helena by 8 June, where he stayed for 12 days. He finally reached the Lizard on 3 September where he learned of the defeat of the Armada five weeks previously. On 10 September 1588 the vessel arrived back in Plymouth after a voyage round the world which had lasted two years and eight weeks, seven months less than the time taken by Drake.

Three years later in August 1591 Cavendish set sail from Plymouth once again, apparently intending to emulate his earlier voyage. His fleet of five ships reached the coast of Brazil at the end of November. On 24 January 1592 the voyage was resumed but Cavendish became separated from the other ships in bad weather and they were not re-united until 18 March. They then set sail for the Straits of Magellan, but the continuing severe weather made the passage hazardous and after struggling half-way through they were obliged to return to the coast of Patagonia with the intention of sailing north to Santos in Brazil. The fleet became separated again, however, on 20 May and after failing to land in Brazil Cavendish set out to return across the Atlantic. He missed St Helena and then, apparently, tried for Ascension Island. Dispirited and ill he continued the voyage north but died during the last stage of the journey and was buried at sea.

The voyages of Drake and Cavendish were both recorded on the Terrestrial Globe, designed by Emery Mollineux and engraved by Jodocus Hondius, which was published with a matching Celestial Globe in London in 1592, the project being financed by William Sanderson, a wealthy London merchant. The two circumnavigations were also indicated in Hondius' 'Drake and Cavendish Map of the World in Two Hemispheres', published at Amsterdam, *c* 1592–3. There can be no doubt that both globes and map provided valuable assistance to later mariners.

This engraving depicts Cavendish at the age of 30.

36 Princess Pocahontas (or Matoaka) (Mrs Rebecca Rolfe) (1595–1617)

American-Indian princess married to an English settler

Facsimile engraving by an unidentified artist after the original print by Simon van de **Passe,** published by W Richardson, 1793.

(O'D 2; copy after Hind: Part II, p.266, 47)

Pocahontas, or Matoaka, was a younger daughter of the Indian chief Powhattan, the so-called 'Emperor of Virginia', to whose territories adjacent to Chesapeake Bay in Virginia came a colony of English settlers in April 1607. This was a second attempt at English colonization in Virginia, for the first colony, established in 1585, had been entirely destroyed – presumably by followers of Powhattan. The newly arrived colonists settled at Jamestown on the James river and became friendly with the local Indians. Prominent among the settlers was Captain John Smith who, in the course of explorations, was captured by the Indians and brought before Powhattan. A romantic version of the encounter has it that Pocahontas was instrumental in saving Smith's life. However that may be Smith certainly succeeded in winning over Powhattan and was eventually sent back to Jamestown under escort. Pocahontas is described as subsequently making frequent journeys to the English settlement, acting as intermediary between her father and the settlers until October 1609 when Smith returned to England.

In the spring of 1612 Captain Samuel Argal, a leading colonist, was trading on the Potomac river and heard that Pocahontas was living in the vicinity. He made contact through her uncle and was eventually successful in luring her aboard his ship. She was then taken hostage for the good behaviour of the Indians towards the settlers and was brought to Jamestown in April 1612. She was well treated and, in the following year, was converted to Christianity, being baptized under the name of Rebecca.

Among the colonists at Jamestown was John Rolfe, originally from Norfolk, and in 1614 he persuaded Pocahontas to marry him, apparently with the agreement of her father. In 1616 Rolfe returned to England, taking with him his wife and child. As a princess she was made much of and received by the queen, even being invited to attend the Twelfth Night masque in 1617. However, the English climate did not suit her and arrangements were made for the return of Pocahontas to Virginia early in the year. Unfortunately she did not live long enough even to start the voyage home and died in March 1617 on board ship off Gravesend. She was buried in St George's Church at Gravesend.

Her husband returned to America, dying there in 1623, having subsequently remarried. The son of John Rolfe and Pocahontas was brought up in London but eventually went to Virginia in 1640. There he married and his descendants married, in due course, into leading Virginian families.

This facsimile, made in the late 18th century, is of Simon van de Passe's portrait made during Pocahontas' London visit of 1616.

The true Picture of m: John Foxe, who Gathered
together and published the Actes and Monuments
of the Church; with an vniuersall History of.
the same, wherein is set at Large the Whole
Course of the Church, from the Primitiue age to these
Latter times, Especially in this Realme of England:
and Scotland.

Martin D sculpsit London. Are to be soulde by Roger Danell

37 E.611–1960

37 John Foxe (1516–1587)

Protestant martyrologist

Engraving by Martin **Droeshout.** A
reversed version of the portrait in Henry
Holland's *Herωologia* of 1620, engraved by
Willem and Magdalena van de **Passe.**

(O'D 5; Hind: Part II, p.352, 6, 1st state)

John Foxe was born at Boston, Lincolnshire,
in 1516. His father died while he was still
young and his mother married again. The
generosity of friends enabled him to go to
Oxford where he was possibly a member of
Brasenose College, although he is not recorded
in the college books. It is likely that he was
later at Magdalen, but once again the records
are defective. He did become, however, a
probationer fellow of Magdalen in 1538 and
a full fellow and lecturer in logic in 1539,
having taken his BA in 1537. He subsequently
became MA in 1543.

He and his friends favoured the more
extreme manifestations of Protestantism and
he refused to attend chapel regularly or to
seek ordination as he was required to do by
the terms of his fellowship. Eventually he felt
obliged to resign, which he did in July 1545.
He then became a tutor with the Lucy family
at Charlecote in Warwickshire and whilst
there married Agnes Randall. Seeking a liveli-
hood he went to London and, after enduring
some hardship, received the patronage of the
Duchess of Richmond who adhered to the
same religious beliefs. Through her influence
he became tutor to the five orphaned children
of the executed Earl of Surrey, brother to the
duchess, and remained with them at Reigate
for five years. During this period Foxe began

to publish his advanced theological writings
and in 1550 he was ordained deacon by
Nicholas Ridley, Bishop of London.

With the accession of Mary in July 1553
the Catholic Duke of Norfolk, grandfather of
the children to whom Foxe was tutor, was
released from prison and swiftly dismissed
him from his post. Foxe found it prudent to
follow many of his Protestant friends to the
continent and eventually made his way,
accompanied by his wife, to Strasburg. He
took with him his manuscript of the first part
of a Latin treatise on the persecution of the
Protestant reformers since the days of William
Wycliffe and this was printed in Strasburg in
1554, being the first of Foxe's publications
dealing with the subject on which his fame
rests. He soon moved on to Frankfurt, where
the largest group of refugee English Protestants lived, and found there a great dispute in
progress between those who agitated for a
more Calvinist form of worship and those
who wished to follow the Anglican liturgy
contained in the second prayer book of
Edward VI. Acrimonious arguments, in which
John Knox was deeply involved, continued
for some time and eventually Foxe moved on
to Basle. There he suffered great poverty until
he found employment as a proof-reader for a
leading Protestant publisher, which seems to
have been the starting point for his future
close connection with the printing trade. He
appears to have become a freeman of the
Stationers' Company of London in 1555 and
commenced his association with the London
printer and publisher John Day.

After the executions of Archbishop Cran-
mer and Bishops Ridley and Latimer, Foxe
composed a plea for tolerance, addressed to
the nobility of England, which was published

at Basle in 1557. He continued to receive reports through his friend Edmund Grindal (later Archbishop of Canterbury) of the continuing persecutions of the English Protestants and it was intended that Foxe should prepare for publication accounts in Latin of the proceedings against the most eminent of these martyrs. This intention was only partly fulfilled, but Grindal urged Foxe to complete his earlier account of the persecutions of the English reformers and by 1559 he had taken the story up to the close of the reign of Mary I (plate 1) who had died the year before. This work, in Latin, was published at Basle in September 1559 and was dedicated to Foxe's former pupil, now Duke of Norfolk. Foxe returned to England in October 1559 and was given hospitality by Norfolk. In January 1560 he was ordained priest by Grindal, now Bishop of London, and commenced work on translating his book into English, spending most of his time at the Duke of Norfolk's house in Aldgate and working with John Day, the printer, at the latter's premises in Aldersgate Street. In March 1563 appeared the first edition of his book in English, entitled *Actes and Monuments* but much better known by its popular title of *Book of Martyrs*. Further editions during Foxe's lifetime appeared in 1570, 1576 and 1583. In 1564 Foxe moved to Day's house and took a prominent role in the printer's business. For a time he seems to have lived at Waltham in Essex, but by about 1570 he had returned to London where he continued to live until his death.

He was made a prebendary of Salisbury Cathedral but was negligent – possibly on conscientious grounds – in the performance of his prescribed duties. He continued to write and to have his books published. One of his major contributions, instigated by the learned Archbishop Matthew Parker, was an edition of the Anglo-Saxon text of the Gospels published in 1571.

In June 1572 Foxe had the sad task of accompanying to the scaffold his friend and former pupil the Duke of Norfolk, who was executed for conspiring with Mary, Queen of Scots, and members of the Catholic nobility against the queen. In the same year Foxe was made a prebendary of Durham but held the office for only a year before resigning. He died in April 1587, after a lengthy period of ill-health, and was buried at St Giles' Church, Cripplegate, with which he had been associated as a clergyman during his years in London. His wife outlived him, not dying until 1605.

Foxe's historical accuracy was questioned both during his lifetime and subsequently and it seems clear that he wrote quickly from a fiercely partisan standpoint, frequently using unchecked material. His book, however, was greatly influential and remained a standard work of reference and edification for the Puritan party for many decades. As a man he is known to have been charitable and of a cheerful disposition despite his great piety.

Ne *pereat totus ROMANI* nominis *Vestis,*
Effigiem turo Sculptor in ære dedit:
Sed melius monumentum, omnis perennius ære
Clare, tibi Ferucis propria, FULCO, manus.

Will.Marshall.sculpsit

Memoriæ clarissimi pariter ac
Doctissimi Viri Dedicavit A.G.

38 E.2398–1960

38 William Fulke
(1538–1589)

Puritan divine, Master of Pembroke Hall, Cambridge

Engraving by William **Marshall**. Frontis-piece to the 1633 edition of Fulke's *The Text of the New Testament of Jesus Christ, translated out of the vulgar Latine by the Papists of the traiterous Seminarie at Rhemes*, originally published in 1589.

(O'D 1; C and N 40)

William Fulke was born in 1538, the son of a wealthy citizen of London. He is said to have been educated at St Paul's School, going from there to St John's College, Cambridge, in 1555. He graduated BA in 1558 and MA in 1563. At his father's wish he studied law for six years in London at Clifford's Inn, but finding the subject not to his taste he returned to Cambridge and a fellowship of his college where he devoted himself to the study of the scriptures, Hebrew and other oriental languages. In 1568 he proceeded to the degree of BD, having previously joined the faction of the Cambridge arch-Puritan Thomas Cartwright and become involved as a leader in the violent dispute over the wearing of vestments which caused great dissension throughout the university. Sir William Cecil (plate 13), chancellor of the university since 1559, was obliged to intervene and Fulke was for a short time deprived of his fellowship, although later reinstated. With the occurrence of another scandalous case, concerned with Fulke's supposed connivance at a technically incestuous marriage, he felt obliged to resign his fellow-ship. After his acquittal in 1569 it was again restored to him and on the vacancy of the mastership of his college in the same year he indulged in a feud with the out-going master, a fellow-Puritan who was seeking re-appointment after resigning his office because he had feared expulsion. The contest became so heated that the Bishop of Ely, as visitor to the college, was invited to intervene with the result that neither of the contestants was able to proceed as a candidate.

By favour of the Earl of Leicester (plate 14), then protector of the Puritan party, Fulke received the chaplaincy to the earl, two livings in East Anglia, the degree of DD and, in May 1578, the mastership of Pembroke Hall (now Pembroke College). Fulke, by this time married, proceeded to augment his stipend as master at the expense of the incomes of other members of the college, and irresponsibly increased its financial responsibilities without achieving any commensurate increase in its income. He promoted the interests of the Puritan cause and was greatly in evidence in public disputation with the adherents and supposed adherents of the Roman Catholic Church. Because of his extreme views he failed to become regius professor of divinity in 1579 but did serve as vice-chancellor of the university in the following year.

The last 10 years of his life saw the production of numerous publications in which he vigorously defended the Puritan position and vehemently attacked the Roman Church. Although a learned and able controversialist his writings are marred by intemperate invective. He was described by a contemporary as 'a pious and learned man, well skilled in history and languages', but the evidence of his career shows him also to have been a violent bigot and an ill-tempered intriguer, a character in marked contrast to that of his successor in the mastership of Pembroke, the saintly Lancelot Andrewes (plate 41).

Fulke died on 28 August 1589 and was buried in the parish church of Dennington, Suffolk, one of the two livings obtained for him by Leicester.

39 William Whitaker (1548–1595)

Puritan divine and Master of St John's College, Cambridge

Engraving by John **Payne** after a portrait at St John's College, Cambridge.

(O'D 1; C and N 34)

William Whitaker was born near Burnley in Lancashire in 1548. His mother's brother, Alexander Nowell, was dean of St Paul's Cathedral, London, and thus, through the interest of his uncle, the boy became a pupil at St Paul's School. With further financial assistance from his uncle he entered Trinity College, Cambridge, in October 1564, becoming, in due course, a scholar of the college and eventually a fellow. He took his BA in 1568 and proceeded to his MA in 1571, becoming well known within the university for his intensive study of the scriptures, the early commentaries on them and the writings of the schoolmen. He found favour with

The right learned Diuine William Whitaker of Trinitie Colledge in Cambridge, and master of St Johns Colledge their. He wrot many learned Bookes against (these English Priests) Stapleton, Sanders, Reignolds, & Campian: as also against that great Arch-Iesuit Robert Bellarmin; he liued godly, was painfull in preaching, and died peaceably. 1595.

Are ſould by Compton Holland ouer againſt the Exchange   Iohn Payne ſculp: London

39 E.3171–1960

John Whitgift (the then Master of Trinity and subsequently Archbishop of Canterbury) and in 1578 he was granted the degree of BD and became a canon of Norwich. In 1580 he was appointed regius professor of divinity in the university and chancellor of St Paul's Cathedral.

He soon became widely known as a defender of the teachings of the Church of England, interpreted in the most Calvinistic sense, and a vigorous opponent of the teachings and practices of the Roman Church.

In 1586 on the recommendation of Cecil (now Lord Burghley) (plate 13) as chancellor of the university, and Whitgift, as archbishop, he was given the crown appointment of the mastership of St John's College which he held until his death. In 1588 he became a DD and in May 1595 was made canon of Canterbury.

Although his appointment as master at first met with some resistance within the college his upright and conscientious discharge of his duties and his impartiality and fair dealing with regard to the various theological factions in the college eventually secured him general respect and affection. He never achieved, however, any major preferment outside the university such as he believed to be his due. This failure may well have been because he was twice married, the queen being strongly opposed to the idea of married bishops.

His controversial writings, like those of his Cambridge contemporary William Fulke at Pembroke (plate 38), were directed against the principal propagandists of the Roman cause. Despite his Calvinist zeal he was, however, widely esteemed for his learning not only in England but also abroad and by some of his theological opponents, notably Cardinal Bellarmine.

Britayne, France, Germany, low-Belgia, Spayne
Doe know thy workes (learn'd Perkins) to thy fame
Marston in warnickeshire, thy birth place knowne,
But Cambridge gaue thee learning, and a Tombe
Thy right hand could not, but thy left hand pen,
Hath almost made thee a wonder vnto men

40   E.1402–1960

40   William Perkins (1558–1602)

Puritan divine and theological writer

Engraving by George **Glover**, after a portrait in Christ's College, Cambridge.

(Not in O'D; C and N 29)

William Perkins serves as an example of a 16th-century teacher who obtained no preferment or lucrative office, either within his university or elsewhere, yet became one of the major intellectual figures of his age. He was born at Marston Jabbett in Warwickshire in 1558 and entered Christ's College, Cambridge, in June 1577 where he was at first notorious for his wildness and drunkenness. However, he experienced a sudden religious conversion and subsequently attached himself to the Puritan party within the university.

In 1584 he took his MA and became a fellow of his college. He was soon appointed lecturer at the Church of Great St Andrew's, just across the street, where the quality of his preaching soon attracted large audiences. His reputation as a Puritan theologian increased rapidly and he was soon in the forefront of the opposition within the university to Anglican ritualistic practices and became a leading defender of such Puritan colleagues as were too zealous in their objections and brought down upon themselves the wrath and punishments of the official Church.

His own writings were strongly Calvinist in character. Nevertheless, his book entitled *A Reformed Catholike*, published in 1597, which attempted to set out clearly the essential points of irreconcilable difference between the Pro-

testant and Catholic faiths, was appreciated for its lucidity of argument by both sides in the controversy. Similarly his skill in marshalling arguments and in adapting his preaching and writing to the abilities of a relatively unsophisticated audience, without in any way abandoning the requirements of accurate scholarship, made him an extremely popular communicator of ideas.

In the autumn of 1594 he resigned his fellowship at Christ's, the probable reason being his marriage which would have obliged him to do so. However, his reputation as a teacher of theology within the university continued to be unequalled and his numerous published works, which cover a wide range of Christian and related topics including the Lord's Prayer, the Apostles' Creed, prophecy, predestination, grace, family life, astrology and witchcraft, attracted a wide readership both during his lifetime and throughout the 17th century. They were translated into many languages as the verses below this engraved portrait testify. They also record the fact that throughout his life he was without the use of his maimed right hand.

Perkins died, much lamented, in 1602, having for many years suffered from the painful affliction of the stone. He was survived by his wife and given a dignified funeral in Great St Andrew's Church at the expense of his college.

This engraving appears, like earlier representations, to be based on a portrait at Christ's College, although the details of the costume differ.

See heer a Shadow from that setting SUNNE,
Whose glorious course through this Horizon runn
Left the dimm face of our dull Hemisphaere,
All one great Eye, all drownd in one great Teare.
Whose rare industrious Soule led his free thought
Through Learning's Universe, and vainly sought
Room for her spacious Selfe; untill at length
She found y̆ way home: with an holy strength

Snatcht herselfe hence to Heav'n; fill'd a bright place
Midst those immortal Fires, and on the face
Of her Great MAKER, fixt a flaming eye,
Where still she reads true, pure Divinitie.
And now y̆ graue Aspect hath deign'd to shrink
Into this lesse appearance. If you think
Tis but a dead face Art doth heer bequeath
Look on the following leaues & see him breath.

Are to be sold by R. Badger dwelling
in Stationer's Hall. 1635.

John Payne Fecit

41   Lancelot Andrewes (1555–1626)

Bishop of Winchester

Engraving by John **Payne**. Frontispiece to Andrewes' *XCVI Sermons*, published in 1632.

(O'D 1; C and N 2, 2nd state)

Lancelot Andrewes, the most celebrated English theologian of his day, was born in Thames Street in the parish of All Hallows, Barking, London, where his father was a merchant who, subsequently, became one of the Masters of Trinity House. From the Merchant Taylors' School he proceeded in 1571 as a Greek scholar to Pembroke Hall (now Pembroke College) in the University of Cambridge. He was elected fellow of his college in 1576 and by the spiritual quality of his theological teaching there attracted much attention within the university. He was ordained into the Church of England in 1580 and later accompanied the Earl of Huntingdon, President of the North, as his chaplain. In the North of England Andrewes' persuasive preaching is said to have won many converts to Anglicanism from the Roman faith. Throughout his life the main elements in his teaching were the enduring catholicity of the English Church, a proposition firmly grounded in his extensive learning in the writings of the Church fathers, and a firm emphasis on the supreme importance for the individual soul of a clear sense of moral duty.

In 1588, through the influence of Sir Francis Walsingham, an old family friend, he became vicar of St Giles', Cripplegate, and soon afterwards a prebendary of St Paul's Cathedral. In

August 1589 he was elected Master of Pembroke Hall on the death of William Fulke (plate 38). Although unable to reside continuously he held the office until 1605 with great benefit to the college, particularly by his establishing its financial affairs on a sound footing.

In London he continued to preach and lecture at both St Giles' and St Paul's and from 1589 to 1609 he was also a prebendary of Southwell Minster. This heavy burden of work, given his conscientious discharge of all duties and his ascetic mode of life, impaired his health so that at one point he became so gravely ill that his life was endangered. On his recovery he was appointed chaplain to Archbishop Whitgift and chaplain in ordinary to the queen. During the queen's reign he refused offers of the sees of Salisbury and Ely because he was unwilling to consent to the required alienation by the crown of part of the revenues of the two dioceses. However, shortly before the queen's death, he did accept first a canonry and later, in 1601, the deanery of Westminster.

On the accession of James I Andrewes received rapid preferment. He was persuaded to accept the bishopric of Chichester in 1605 and in the same year he was appointed almoner to the king. In 1609 he removed to the bishopric of Ely and was also appointed to the Privy Council and, finally, in 1619, he was appointed Bishop of Winchester. Previously, in March 1611, George Abbot, then Bishop of London, became Archbishop of Canterbury, an office which many people had expected to be offered to Andrewes. This disappointment was apparently not shared by him, for he displayed no resentment at being passed over.

He had taken part with great distinction in the Hampton Court Conference of 1603–4 where his great learning had been of considerable service in rejecting the Puritan claims and in stemming the advance of Calvinism in the Church of England. In 1607 he was among those scholars appointed to prepare the new translation of the Bible, now known as the Authorized Version or King James' Bible. His scholarship was held in universal esteem in England and he was one of the few English theologians of the day who was known to and respected by European scholars. He was reputed to be skilled in 15 languages, with especial skill in oriental languages, and his knowledge of the writings of the Church fathers was unequalled. He remained, however, a simple, modest and gentle man with a marked sense of humour, noted for his generous benefactions and for his scrupulous care in seeking to give preferment only to deserving and worthy men. Of this latter concern as Bishop of Winchester John Aubrey remarks that 'he ordered (his bishopric) with great prudence as to government of the parsons, preferring of ingenious persons that were staked to poor livings and did waste away. He made it his enquiry to find out such men'.

As a preacher he was admired for his spirituality, his learning, his eloquence and his charm of delivery. For more than 15 years he was the required preacher at court at the great festivals of the Church and during the penitential seasons. Bishop Andrewes' personal manual of private devotions and his devotions to be used on behalf of the sick and at Holy Communion were published after his death and quickly became widely used devotional works.

Despite his considerable influence on his age through his scholarship and his example of personal saintliness Bishop Andrewes' major contribution to his church and to his king during his lifetime may be found in his reasoned defence of the Church of England against the attacks of her Puritan and Roman Catholic opponents. A reluctant controversialist, and always moderate and just in his assessments of arguments and personalities, his voice was heard with respect and to good effect, notably in response to the attacks of Cardinal Bellarmine.

He died on 25 September 1626 at his official London residence, Winchester House in Southwark, and was buried in St Saviour's Church (now Southwark Cathedral) where his splendid tomb remains. A pleasant tribute was paid by his friend John Hacket, later Bishop of Lichfield, who enquired, 'Who could come near the shrine of such a saint and not offer up a few grains of glory upon it?'

This engraving is from a portrait by an unidentified artist in the Bodleian Library, Oxford, representing Andrewes in old age.

42 E.3636–1960

42 Robert Parsons
(1546–1610)

Jesuit missionary and controversialist

Engraving by Jean **Waldor I.**

(O'D 2)

Robert Parsons was born in Nether Stowey, Somerset, on 24 June 1546, his father being said to have been a blacksmith. He was educated in Somerset and from the free school at Taunton he went on to Oxford in 1564, being first at St Mary's Hall and later at Balliol College. He took his BA in 1568 and was elected a fellow of his college in the same year. He was admitted to his MA degree in 1572 and subsequently became bursar and then dean of Balliol. He twice took the oath of royal supremacy, but failed to seek Anglican ordination as the terms of his fellowship required. Although popular as a teacher he quarrelled with his senior colleagues and, as a result, left Balliol early in 1574.

Later that year he left England for Italy, intending to study medicine at the University of Padua. It is believed that while on his journey he was received into the Roman Catholic Church at Louvain. After only a few months at Padua he travelled to Rome and offered himself as a novice to the Society of Jesus. On acceptance he commenced his novitiate on 24 July 1575 and was eventually ordained priest in 1578.

After lengthy discussions it was decided that Parsons and another Jesuit, Father Edmund Campion, should go into England as missionaries and auxiliaries to the secular clergy. The Jesuit order was greatly concerned that this action should not be construed by the English Government as having a political connotation and Parsons and Campion were strictly enjoined not to become involved in affairs of state. They landed in England in June 1580 and Parsons soon made many converts during a missionary tour. The authorities, alarmed by these activities, brought in fresh penalties against those who harboured priests, with the result that Parsons was obliged to seek refuge in the house of the Spanish ambassador. From this point began his real involvement in political intrigue, a process encouraged by the torture of captured priests and the imprisonment of Catholic laymen. Parsons boldly established a secret printing press from which he issued several controversial pamphlets for distribution in England. Parliament responded in March 1581 by making reconciliation to the Church of Rome a treasonable offence and greatly increasing the fines for recusancy. In July of that year Edmund Campion was betrayed, captured and put to death. Parsons found it necessary to leave the country and in the autumn he escaped to France.

From then until the defeat of the Armada in 1588 Parsons was in constant communication with the Duke of Guise, Philip of Spain, the Pope and the Duke of Parma fostering plans at first for the invasion of Scotland and afterwards for the invasion of England. In 1588 he served briefly as rector of the English College in Rome, but in November of that year he went to Spain where he remained (with visits to Portugal) for nearly nine years. He was concerned with the business of the Jesuit Order, notably in the establishment in Spain under royal protection of English seminaries and communities of secular priests. He also continued to urge Philip II to renew his attack upon England in order to win back the country for the Catholic cause. In a proclamation of November 1591 Elizabeth named him as a principal agent in renewed invasion projects. In 1594 he published a book dealing with the question of the succession to the English crown on the death of Elizabeth in which he proposed the Infanta of Spain as the most suitable successor. The English Parliament responded by declaring possession of the book to be high treason and many English Catholics came to view it with dismay.

Parson's old friend Cardinal Allen died in Rome in 1594 and Parsons was suspected, probably unjustly, of wishing to succeed him in his cardinalate. Much intrigue and dissension had developed amongst the English Catholics since the execution of Mary, Queen of Scots, in 1587 and there was a double distrust of Parsons' Spanish intrigues and of undue Jesuit influence in England. There was even dissension amongst the students of the English College at Rome and Parsons felt it essential for him to return there to restore order. He was re-appointed rector of the college, a post he continued to hold until his death. He was also instrumental in securing the appointment of George Blackwell as archpriest (rather than as bishop) in England, with an obligation on Blackwell's part to consult with the English Jesuit superior Henry Garnett (plate 43) in all major ecclesiastical matters. This move was greatly resented by the secular clergy who sought to present in Rome their case against this arrangement and to press for the establishment of episcopal government. In 1600 a group of English secular priests appealed directly to the Pope and Parsons was repeatedly attacked in various books by Catholic authors which were secretly printed in England. The outcome was that the archpriest was forbidden to consult with the Jesuits in the affairs of the secular clergy. Whilst in Rome Parsons had been trying to interest Pope Clement VIII in various marriage schemes directed towards securing a Catholic successor to the English throne. However, once James I was seen to be securely established on the throne he accepted the fact and immediately prior to the Gunpowder Plot was urging Father Garnett to restrain any proposals for attempted rebellion.

Parsons' last years were spent principally in Rome as prefect of the Jesuit mission and rector of the English College. He engaged himself eagerly in theological controversy and his writings are notable for their clarity and vigour. He died in Rome on 15 April 1610 and was buried in the church of the English College. His ambition had been to see the restoration of Roman Catholicism in England, either by persuasion or by force, and all his great energy was directed towards that end. In personal appearance he has been described as 'of middle size, his complexion rather swarthy, which, with strong features, made his countenance somewhat forbidding'. This engraving is said to represent Parsons in the last year of his life, when aged 64.

Si quid patimini propter iustitiam, beati.i.petri.
Henricus Garnetus anglus e societate IESV passus
3 May 1606. JOHAN WIERICX EXCVD CVM (…) ET PRIVILL HS D (…)

43 E.3884–1960

43 Henry Garnett (1555–1606)

Jesuit missionary

Engraving by Johan **Wierix.**

(Not in O'D)

Henry Garnett was born in 1555 at Heanor in Derbyshire, the son of a respected schoolmaster. He was brought up as a Protestant and became a scholar of Winchester College, where it is thought he became converted to the Roman Catholic faith. He did not proceed to New College, Oxford, as might normally have been expected of a Winchester scholar, going instead to London where he began to study law while working as a printer's proof-reader. He stayed there for two years until he finally resolved to devote himself fully to the service of his church. With a companion he made his way to Rome, where he became a Jesuit novice on 11 September 1575. He was highly regarded by his teachers at the Roman College and became skilled in all branches of learning, his proficiency in mathematics and Hebrew being particularly esteemed. Indeed such was his mathematical skill that he was detained in Rome as a teacher and prevented for at least two years from travelling to England as a missionary as he wished to do. He finally left Rome for England on 8 May 1586, travelling with Father Robert South-well. The two priests arrived safely early in July and joined Father William Weston, at that time the only Jesuit priest serving in England. Weston was soon to be imprisoned in Wisbech Castle and Garnett was then appointed to succeed him as Jesuit superior in England. During the years of his ministry he secured many converts to Roman Catholicism and at the time of his death there were no less than 40 Jesuits serving in the English mission.

Garnett lived in various Catholic houses, moving on whenever prudence dictated a change. Amongst these addresses was a house called White Webbs in Enfield Chase and it so chanced that at the time of the arrest of Guy Fawkes (plate 31) in November 1605 a letter was found in his possession addressed to that house. Garnett was known to have been living there until shortly before the discovery of the Gunpowder Plot and Robert Cecil (by then Lord Salisbury) was anxious to discover as much as possible about the plot and those involved in it, especially from those priests who had acted as confessors to the conspira-tors. Of the three so involved Fathers Green-way and Gerard managed to escape abroad but Garnett was eventually captured at Hind-lip Hall, near Worcester, where he had remained hidden in a secret 'priest's hole' for four days. He was taken to London as a prisoner, being well treated on Lord Salis-bury's instructions. He and another priest captured with him, Father Thomas Oldcorne, were examined by the Privy Council and sent to the Tower. Further numerous examinations took place before the Council but Garnett made no confession of his involvement in the plot. As the king had expressly forbidden the use of torture against him his jailers contrived to allow him to speak with Oldcorne on five occasions in a situation where all that was said could be overheard and recorded by Salis-bury's men.

During his testimony Garnett admitted that the conspirator Robert Catesby (plate 31) had asked him for his opinion as to whether or not any enterprise to forward the cause of Roman Catholicism could be lawful if it involved the deaths of innocent people and that he, Garnett, without knowing anything of the circumstances envisaged in the hypo-thetical case had agreed that such action could be considered lawful. He also admitted that he became aware of the details of the plot from Father Greenway through the confes-sional. Greenway had likewise received his information through Catesby's sacramental confession. His transmission of the details to Garnett was with Catesby's consent and on the understanding that if the plot were to be discovered by other means Garnett was to be at liberty to disclose the truth. Both priests had been shocked to learn of the plot and, bound to silence as they were, had attempted to dissuade the conspirators from violent action.

At his trial at Guildhall on 28 March 1606 Garnett pleaded in his defence that he was not involved in the plot and only knew of it through the privileged channel of the confes-sional where his priestly function prevented him from revealing the secret which had been confided to him. This plea was disregarded and Garnett was sentenced to be hanged,. drawn and quartered. The execution was car-ried out in St Paul's Churchyard on 3 May 1606.

With regard to Garnett's appearance it is of interest to quote an official description, given in a proclamation seeking his arrest, which states him to have been 'of a middling stature, full-faced, fat of body, of complexion fair, his forehead high on each side, with a little thin hair coming down upon the middest of the fore part of his head; the hair of his head and beard griseled'.

This engraving presumably represents Gar-nett as he appeared at the time of his execution.